Best Easy Day Hikes
Anchorage

Help Us Keep This Guide Up to Date

Every effort has been made by the author and editors to make this guide as accurate and useful as possible. However, many things can change after a guide is published—trails are rerouted, regulations change, techniques evolve, facilities come under new management, etc.

We appreciate hearing from you concerning your experiences with this guide and how you feel it could be improved and kept up to date. While we may not be able to respond to all comments and suggestions, we'll take them to heart and we'll also make certain to share them with the author. Please send your comments and suggestions to the following address:

FalconGuides
Reader Response/Editorial Department
Falconeditorial@rowman.com

Thanks for your input, and happy trails!

Best Easy Day Hikes Series

Best Easy Day Hikes
Anchorage

Second Edition

John Tyson

FALCON GUIDES

ESSEX, CONNECTICUT

FALCONGUIDES®

An imprint of Globe Pequot, the trade division of The Rowman &
Littlefield Publishing Group, Inc.
4501 Forbes Blvd., Ste. 200
Lanham, MD 20706
www.rowman.com

Falcon and FalconGuides are registered trademarks and Make Adventure Your Story is a trademark of The Rowman & Littlefield Publishing Group, Inc.

Distributed by NATIONAL BOOK NETWORK

British Library Cataloguing in Publication Information available

Library of Congress Cataloging-in-Publication Data
ISBN 978-1-4930-6636-0 (paper: alk. paper)
ISBN 978-1-4930-6637-7 (electronic)

∞™ The paper used in this publication meets the minimum requirements of American National Standard for Information Sciences—Permanence of Paper for Printed Library Materials, ANSI/NISO Z39.48-1992.

Contents

Urban Anchorage Trails

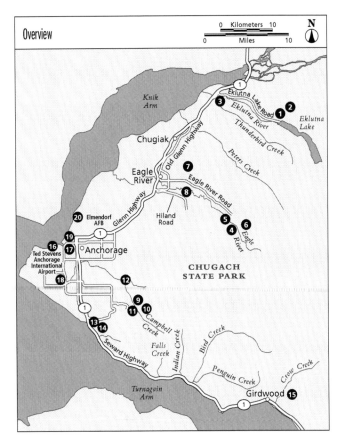

Meet Your Guide

John Tyson has been a freelance photographer/author and writer since 1996. His lifelong love of nature and the outdoors is evidenced by his work for many national magazines, calendars, and book publishers. John and his wife Madelyn have been traveling and hiking in North America and internationally for over twenty years. He is a longtime beekeeper, and enjoys biking, birding, travel, and trekking the endless amazing trails of Alaska's Chugach State Park and Anchorage, Alaska.

Introduction

Most hiking around Anchorage is done in Chugach State Park, our country's third-largest state park, which encompasses nearly 500,000 acres of wilderness. It is the largest park in North America within an urban setting, sitting immediately east of Anchorage, the largest city in Alaska. There are several trail systems located within Anchorage's city parks, but a majority of the trails are in the Chugach Mountains.

The trails in Chugach State Park can provide you with a variety of wilderness experiences and can accommodate the skill level of most any hiker, often depending on how far you want to hike. The opportunities for adventure are endless. Stunning alpine lakes, icy glaciers, and a 5,000-foot elevation rise add to the natural wonder of Chugach State Park. Nature and wildlife are abundant in the park, and you won't be disappointed. World-class wildlife viewing or afternoon berry picking is available just minutes from downtown Anchorage. Mountain streams offer opportunities for fishing and even recreational gold panning.

On a clear day, Mount McKinley (Denali) and the Alaska Range can be seen to the north, the smaller Tordrillo Mountain range to the west–northwest, the Chugach Mountains to the east, the Talkeetna Mountains to the west, the Kenai Mountains to the south, and the volcanic Chigmit Mountains of the Aleutian Range to the southwest. Cook Inlet sits west of Anchorage and is visible from several trails within the park.

The trails presented in this guide provide a mere glimpse of the wilderness opportunities Chugach has to offer and the outstanding trail systems within Anchorage itself. This guide can get you started on your own road to adventure and will introduce you to some of the most picturesque areas of Alaska—true Alaskan wilderness and hiking trails unrivaled anywhere else in the United States.

The trails range from easy to moderate, based on steepness, and can take anywhere from 30 minutes to a full day, with optional extensions. Many of the trails in the Chugach Mountains will allow you to choose your hiking distance according to your personal time schedule, so you can explore as far as you want to go.

Weather

The Anchorage area has four seasons and a relatively mild winter. This maritime climate allows the park to be utilized year-round. The park itself receives 160 inches of rain annually in the extreme southeast and only 12 inches per year in the northeast. Keep these extremes in mind as you plan your hike.

When you come to Alaska, dress for changeable weather. That means wearing layers. You will want to be able to peel them off or put them on as conditions warrant. The weather can change quickly, abruptly, and often, going from sunny and warm to cool and damp within a matter of minutes. Different regions of Chugach—even different areas of the city of Anchorage—can experience significant differences in weather, so always take the weather into account when planning your hike.

Summers here are like nowhere else in the world. Unlike many other places, you do not need to restrict your hiking to early morning or late afternoon because of high temperatures and high humidity. In July Anchorage temperatures average a daytime high of 65 degrees Fahrenheit and a nighttime low of 51 degrees, with very low humidity. You will experience cooler temperatures in the mountains, depending on altitude. On the day of the summer solstice (June 21), there are twenty-four hours of functional daylight. Long summer days provide plenty of daylight hours for hiking. Winter days are much shorter. The winter solstice (December 21), the shortest day of the year, provides only 5 hours and 28 minutes of daylight in this area.

Flora and Fauna

Animals such as brown and black bears, moose, wolves, porcupines, foxes, snowshoe hares, martens, squirrels, and lynx are all common in the area. There is also a diverse mix of birds, including juncos, pine grosbeaks, sparrows, common redpolls, chickadees, nuthatches, owls, goshawks, woodpeckers, spruce grouse, willow ptarmigan, and jays.

When hiking in Alaska, even within Anchorage's city limits, you are hiking in bear country. This part of Alaska has both black and brown bears, and you cannot identify them merely by color. Study the differences in bears, learn about bear behavior, and be bear-aware as you hike, making noise (you never want to surprise a bear) and traveling in pairs or groups. Every hike has the possibility of a bear encounter, so learn how to react before you head out on the trail.

Moose are another large animal often encountered on area trails. They are not tame. Respect their size and space, particularly when they have calves with them. Wait for them to clear the trail, or make a large circle around them. Moose injure more people than bears each year in Alaska.

Preparing for Your Hike

The variety of ecosystems, habitats, and terrains in Chugach State Park makes hiking here an extraordinary and rewarding experience. Hiking here will create a desire for adventure and exploration, and will leave you with a strong admiration for and a unique connection with the park's awesome beauty and vastness.

Because of the extremes in terrain and weather variances, it's important to be well prepared on every hike. The following tips can help ensure an enjoyable trek:

- Again, be sure to dress in layers. It is far better to have to take off a layer because you're too warm than to be cold and risk hypothermia.
- Be prepared for rain, even on sunny days.
- Carry a first-aid kit, compass, mosquito repellent, sunscreen, and plenty of water, even on short hikes.
- Study a map of the area and the general trail terrain you will be traveling.

Wilderness Restrictions and Regulations

Alaska's Division of Parks and Outdoor Recreation is dedicated to preserving the wilderness of Alaska's Chugach State Park and helping you discover the unique features the park has to offer. Although overnight trip plans are not a requirement, they are suggested, and can be filed with the rangers at Chugach State Park Headquarters.

There are various rules for different outdoor sports within the park. However, hikers should be aware of the following regulations while using the park:

- Fireworks are not permitted in the park. They can be dangerous to other visitors, disturb wildlife, and cause fires.

- Drone flying is not permitted anywhere in the park.

- Berries and edible plants can be gathered for personal consumption but not for sale. Other natural items, such as rocks, trees, and vegetation, should not be disturbed.

- Fires are allowed in portable camp stoves, metal fire rings provided by the park, and on the gravel beds of the Eklutna River, Peters and Bird Creeks, and the main stem of the Eagle River at times of low water. Random campfires can cause scars that last for decades.

- Wood that is dead and lying on the ground can be used for fires in park-provided fire pits.

- Gold panning is allowed year-round, except in streams that support salmon. Only a pan and shovel may be used. No motorized equipment or chemicals are allowed.

- Guns and other weapons may be carried for self-protection.

- No target practice is allowed. During hunting seasons, guns may not be discharged within 0.5 mile of any campground, picnic area, ski area, or roadway in the park, including the Seward Highway.

- Hunting and fishing are permitted during legal seasons. Hunting and fishing licenses are required. Contact the Alaska Department of Fish and Game, 333 Raspberry Road, Anchorage 99518; (907) 267-2257.

- Mudflats are located in the intertidal areas along Turnagain Arm. Even though they look inviting to explore, they are extremely dangerous. The solid surface of the glacial muds can suddenly change to quicksand. Many people and animals have become trapped in the mud and drowned due to rapidly rising tides. STAY OFF THE MUDFLATS.

- Dogs must be kept on a leash at all visitor centers and campgrounds; barking is not permitted after 11 p.m. On some trails in this guide, dogs can be under voice control once on the trail. However, be aware that porcupines, moose, bears, and other natural elements can endanger the safety of both pet and owner.

- Vehicles must remain on the roadway, in designated parking areas, or on camping pads. Posted speed limits and parking regulations are enforced.

Trail Contacts

For park regulations and other park information, check out https://dnr.alaska.gov/parks/index.htm. The following trail contacts and organizations can provide additional information to help you plan your hike:

Alaska Department of Natural Resources Public Information Center: Atwood Building, 550 West Seventh Avenue, Suite 1360, Anchorage 99501; (907) 269-8400; http://dnr.alaska.gov/commis/pic/

Alaska Public Lands Information Center: 605 West Fourth Avenue, Suite 105, Anchorage 99501; (907) 644-3661; https://www.nps.gov/anch/index.htm

Anchorage District Office: 4700 BLM Road, Anchorage 99507; (907) 267-1246 https://www.blm.gov/office/anchorage-district-office

Anchorage Park Foundation: 3201 C Street, Suite 111, Anchorage 99503; (907) 274-1003; https://

anchorageparkfoundation.org/; e-mail: info@anchorageparkfoundation.org.

Anchorage Visitor Information Center: 546 West Fourth Avenue, Anchorage 99501; (907) 257-2363; www.anchorage.net

Campbell Creek Science Center: 5600 Science Center Drive, Anchorage 99507; (907) 267-1247; https://www.blm.gov/learn/interpretive-centers/campbell-creek-science-center

Chugach National Forest: 3301 C Street, Suite 300, Anchorage 99503; (909) 743-9500; https://www.fs.usda.gov/chugach

Chugach State Park Headquarters: Potter Section House State Historic Site, Mile 115 Seward Highway (mailing address: 18620 Seward Highway, Anchorage 99516); (907) 345-5014; http://dnr.alaska.gov/parks/index.htm; e-mail: dnr.pic@alaska.gov. Park headquarters is open Monday through Friday 10 a.m. to 4:30 p.m.

Eagle River Nature Center: 32750 Eagle River Road, Eagle River 99577; (907) 694-2108; www.ernc.org

Zero Impact

Anchorage's trails are heavily used year-round. We, as trail users and advocates, must be especially vigilant to make sure our passing leaves no lasting mark. Here are some basic guidelines for preserving trails in the region:

- Pack out all your own trash, including biodegradable items like orange peels. You might also pack out garbage left by less considerate hikers.

- Don't approach or feed any wild creatures—the ground squirrel eyeing your snack food is best able to survive if it remains self-reliant.
- Don't pick wildflowers or gather rocks, antlers, feathers, and other treasures along the trail. Removing these items will only take away from the next hiker's backcountry experience.
- Avoid damaging trailside soils and plants by remaining on the established route. This is also a good rule of thumb for avoiding devil's club and cow parsnip, common trailside irritants.

How to Use This Guide

The at-a-glance information at the beginning of each hike includes a short description, the hike distance in miles and type of trail (loop, out and back, or shuttle), the time required for an average hiker, difficulty rating, elevation gain, the trail surface, the best season for hiking the trail, other trail users, whether dogs are allowed on the hike, applicable fees or permits, maps, trail contacts for additional information, and any special considerations. Directions to the trailhead are also provided, along with a general description of what you'll see along the way. A detailed route finder sets forth mileages between significant landmarks along the trail.

Be aware that Alaska Highway 1 is called the Glenn Highway north of Anchorage and the Seward Highway south of Anchorage. Those are the names that will be used in this book.

A Note on GPS Coordinate Formats

The degree, minutes, and seconds format (e.g., 41° 24'1 2.2" N 2° 10' 26.5" E) will not automatically work with some applications, such as Google Earth, which may require decimal degrees (e.g., 41.40338, 2.17403").

Check to see what your application uses before using the GPS coordinates provided, and if necessary, you may convert those coordinates online using a GPS converter. There are many online converters that are free to use.

Here's an example of how to convert GPS coordinates:

GPS: N35° 49' 56" / W106° 38' 34"

Find your conversion website.

Type this into "latitude": N35° 49' 56"

Then type this into "longitude": W106° 38' 34"

Hit "calculate."

Down below you will see:

Degrees Lat Long: 35.8322222°,-106.6427778°

Copy/paste 35.8322222°,-106.6427778° into Google Earth and hit "search."

It will then take you to the location.

Trail Finder

Best Hikes for Dogs

Best Hikes for Waterfalls

Best Hikes for the Entire Family

Best Hikes for Great Views

Best Hikes for Nature Lovers

4	Albert Loop Trail
5	Rodak Nature Trail
6	Dew Mound Trail
13	Potter Marsh Wildlife Viewing Boardwalk Trail
15	Winner Creek Trail
19	Tony Knowles Coastal Trail

Best Hikes for Streams and Rivers

4	Albert Loop Trail
5	Rodak Nature Trail
15	Winner Creek Trail
17	Lanie Fleischer Chester Creek Trail
18	Campbell Creek Trail
19	Tony Knowles Coastal Trail

Best Hikes for Lakes

1	Eklutna Lakeside Trail
6	Dew Mound Trail
17	Lanie Fleischer Chester Creek Trail
19	Tony Knowles Coastal Trail

Best Hikes for Geology Lovers

4	Albert Loop Trail
6	Dew Mound Trail
16	Earthquake Park / Inside the Slide Trail

Best Hikes for Viewing Gorges

3	Thunderbird Falls Trail
15	Winner Creek Trail

Map Legend

═○═	State Highway
═══	Local Roads
═ ═ ═ ═	Unimproved Road
- - - - - -	Trail
▬▬▬▬▬	Featured Route
┣━┿━┿━┫	Railroad
──────	River/Creek
▬▬▬	Lake/Ocean
▭	State Park
≍	Bridge
▲	Campground
•—•	Gate
❷	Information
℗	Parking
▲	Peak
⊞	Picnic Area
■	Point of Interest/Other Trailhead
⊞	Restroom
‖‖‖‖‖	Steps
❻	Trailhead
○	Town
≷	Waterfall
◧	Viewpoint
N ⊕	True North (Magnetic North is approximately 15.5° East)

North of Anchorage

1 Eklutna Lakeside Trail

This popular trail is utilized year-round by local Alaskans, with most every type of outdoor recreational activity available and extraordinary foliage colors in the fall. It is well traveled, extremely scenic, and allows for various means of travel. Although nearly 13 miles long, it is easy to follow, and you can walk as little or as much as you like. It follows the Eklutna Lake shoreline and passes waterfalls and steep canyon walls. Wildlife such as bears, moose, Dall sheep, mountain goats, and numerous bird species are prominent in the area.

Distance: 12.7 miles one-way
Approximate hiking time: As little or as long as you wish
Difficulty: Easy
Elevation gain: 300 feet
Trail surface: Gravel road
Best season: Year-round; campgrounds open May 1 through September 30
Other trail users: Equestrians, cyclists, skiers, snowmobilers
Canine compatibility: Leashed dogs permitted
Fees and permits: Parking fee

Maps: USGS Anchorage; Imus Geographics Chugach State Park map (www.imusgeographics.com)
Trail contacts: Chugach State Park Headquarters, Potter Section House State Historic Site, Mile 115 Seward Highway (mailing address: 18620 Seward Highway, Anchorage 99516); (907) 345-5014; http://dnr.alaska.gov/parks/index.htm; e-mail: dnr.pic@alaska.gov. Park headquarters is open Monday through Friday 10 a.m. to 4:30 p.m.
Special considerations: None

Finding the trailhead: From Anchorage travel 25 miles north on the Glenn Highway. Take the Thunderbird Falls exit and follow the road to the right. Drive beyond the Thunderbird Falls trailhead and parking lot on your right and cross the Eklutna River. Just after crossing the river, turn right onto Eklutna Lake Road and continue 10 miles to the pay station and Eklutna Lake. There are two large day-use parking lots. If you're coming from the north side of the parking lots, cross a small bridge and turn right at the main trailhead. GPS: N61 24.622 / W149 08.103

The Hike

The Eklutna Lakeside Trail follows the shoreline of Eklutna Lake. Seven miles long, the lake offers unspoiled beauty and recreation year-round. It is a beautiful setting, and you can hike as far as you desire or have the time for.

The trail is basically a gravel road, but it is in good condition. The road is easily hiked and biked and is also popular with ATV riders. But don't let the ATV traffic discourage you from the hike; they won't be in your way. The trail branches often, with high-road and low-road routes. The high road is intended for the ATVs; the low route is a much narrower trail intended for hikers, and will take you on a more intimate walk along the shoreline. These frequent forks along the trail are very well marked and easily identified. The first fork appears at Mile 1.0. Veer right onto a narrow trail; the ATVs will take the high, wide road straight ahead.

At 2.65 miles you come to the first stream crossing and bridge. The stream is called Yuditna Creek. After the bridge, the trail makes an abrupt right-hand turn back toward the lake. (FYI: Another right turn will take you to one of the park's public-use cabins—the Yuditna Creek Cabin, with an outstanding view of the lake. Cabins are available by reservation only and are very popular, so plan well in advance if you want to use one. Please respect others' privacy if the cabin is occupied.)

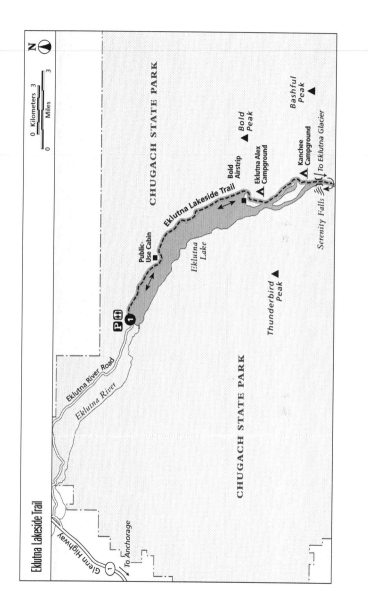

Pass the trail to the cabin and continue to follow the lake shoreline. Cross Bold Creek at approximately 4.8 miles. There is an excellent waterfall on the north side of the bridge and a picturesque view as the creek enters the lake on the south side. Just after you cross the bridge, a trailhead marks the access point to Bold Ridge Trail on your left. This is a steep 3.5-mile one-way trip.

After the turnoff to Bold Ridge, the Eklutna Lakeside Trail narrows and follows a steep gravelly ridge along the lake. You'll come to a third creek, 8-Mile Creek, at approximately 7.7 miles. This is at the far south end of the lake. The trail starts heading in a westerly direction and then turns south again.

Just after crossing the creek, pass a route on your right that goes to Bold Airstrip. Continue on the main trail that winds to your left. Pay attention to the steep ledges on your left as you continue traveling along the glacial gravel bar. A pair of binoculars will come in handy for spotting Dall sheep on the rocky ledges.

At 8.4 miles come to the first campground, Eklutna Alex Campground, with picnic tables, primitive campsites, and restroom facilities. Just remember that since this is bear country, there is no trash service. What you pack in you need to pack out. At Mile 10.0 the trailhead for East Fork Trail, which leads to Tulchina Falls, is on your left.

You will encounter one other campground, Kanchee Campground, along the trail at Mile 11.0. Both Eklutna Alex and Kanchee Campgrounds are good places to camp when making this an overnight trip. The Serenity Falls public-use cabin is another alternative for overnight stays. The cabin is located between Miles 11.0 and 12.0, and access is on the path that travels straight ahead. Turn right to stay on the main trail. Cross a large bridge with a view of two large waterfalls.

Continue on the main trail to reach Serenity Falls at approximately 11.5 miles. The trail becomes very rocky, with large, loose stones, and heads uphill. If you are on bikes, you will probably need to tie up and secure your bikes somewhere along the path, or else walk them from here to the river shoreline. Reach the end of the trail at 12.7 miles, where a large, flat boulder overlooks the river.

Miles and Directions

0.0 Start at the trailhead signpost in front of the rental concession building.

1.0 Veer right and follow the trail along the lakeshore. (FYI: ATVs go straight ahead.)

2.65 Cross the bridge over Yuditna Creek and continue to follow the lakeshore. (Option: Turn right to reach the public-use cabin at 2.75 miles.)

4.8 Cross Bold Creek on a bridge and pass the Bold Ridge Trail on your left. (Option: Bold Ridge is a steep, 3.5-mile, one-way trail.)

7.7 Cross 8-Mile Creek.

8.0 Pass the route to Bold Airstrip on the right.

8.4 Reach Eklutna Alex Campground.

10.0 Pass the East Fork trailhead on your left and cross the bridge over the East Fork Eklutna River. (Option: Follow the East Fork Trail 4.0 miles one-way to Tulchina Falls.)

11.0 Pass the Kanchee Campground. (FYI: Kanchee means "porcupine" in Athapaskan.)

11.5 Turn right and cross a large bridge with views of two water-falls. Proceed straight ahead to the Serenity Falls public-use cabin.

11.8 Arrive at Serenity Falls.

12.7 Arrive at the riverbank and end of the trail. (Option: You can walk another 0.3 mile along the river to the Eklutna Glacier overlook. Unfortunately, the glacier has receded from this point.)

2 Eydlu Bena Loop Trail

This is a good hike if your time is limited or if you came to the park for biking or spending an afternoon at the lake and want another activity. The trail is well marked and easy to follow, with relatively low elevation gain, making it ideal for the entire family. It can also be hiked in early spring when other trails are still closed.

Distance: 2.0-mile loop
Approximate hiking time: 1 to 2 hours
Difficulty: Easy
Elevation gain: 300 feet
Trail surface: Dirt road, gravel
Best season: Summer through fall
Other trail users: Skiers
Canine compatibility: Leashed dogs permitted
Fees and permits: Parking fee
Maps: USGS Anchorage; Imus Geographics Chugach State Park map (www.imusgeographics.com)

Trail contacts: Chugach State Park Headquarters, Potter Section House State Historic Site, Mile 115 Seward Highway (mailing address: 18620 Seward Highway, Anchorage 99516); (907) 345-5014; http://dnr.alaska.gov/parks/index.htm; e-mail: dnr.pic@alaska.gov. Park headquarters is open Monday through Friday 10 a.m. to 4:30 p.m.
Special considerations: None

Finding the trailhead: From Anchorage travel 25 miles north on the Glenn Highway. Take the Thunderbird Falls exit and follow the road to the right. Drive 0.3 mile beyond the Thunderbird Falls trailhead and parking lot on your right and cross the bridge. Just after crossing the river, turn right onto Eklutna Lake Road and travel 10 miles to the pay station and Eklutna Lake. There are two large day-use parking lots. From the north side of the lots, cross a small bridge and turn left at the main trail marker. The Eydlu Bena trailhead is just ahead on your right. GPS: N61 24.611 / W149 07.503

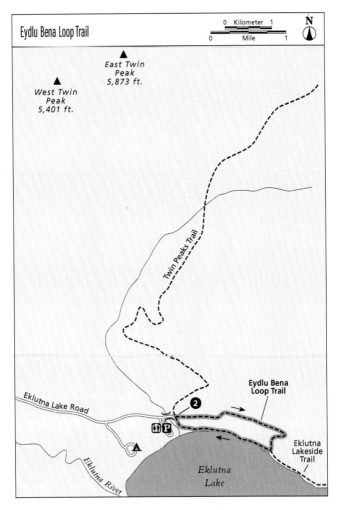

The Hike

Eydlu Bena Loop Trail is an easy, forested walk. It begins on a wide old roadbed, narrows into a dirt gravel path, and eventually loops down to join the Eklutna Lakeside Trail.

After leaving the parking lot, locate the main trailhead and signpost in front of the park's equipment rental building. Turn left and walk about 100 feet; the Eydlu Bena Trail begins on your right.

The trail starts out on a dirt road. At about 0.3 mile from the trailhead, leave the road; veer left, and continue heading uphill. This is probably the steepest portion of the trail. The trail travels through a spruce-hardwood forest inhabited by black and brown bears, moose, porcupines, and both red and northern flying squirrels. Although you won't always see the animals themselves, their signs along the trail are often evident. After approximately 1 mile a trail post directs you to the right and downhill to the Eklutna Lakeside Trail. This is the trail you want. The path on the left is an unmaintained trail that continues upward through a tunnel of trees, eventually dead-ending at a rocky boulder area often used by Dall sheep ewes to lamb in spring.

Turn right at the signpost and loop back down toward Eklutna Lake. Views of the lake become apparent as you hike downhill. The Eydlu Bena Trail joins the lakeside trail at approximately 1.25 miles. Turn right at this junction and follow the road along the shoreline back to the parking lot.

Miles and Directions

0.0 Start at the main trailhead in front of the equipment rental building and go left. The trail begins just past the building on the right.

0.9 Turn right at the trail marker post and head downhill.

1.25 Reach the junction with the Eklutna Lakeside Trail. Turn right onto the gravel road and head back toward the parking lot.

2.0 Arrive back at the trailhead.

3 Thunderbird Falls Trail

This short and relatively easy hike through one of Alaska's scenic deciduous forests takes you to a viewing deck above a steep gorge with views of East and West Twin Peaks and the Eklutna River below. In another half-mile, a second platform affords an unobstructed view of historic Thunderbird Falls. An optional side trail takes you down to Thunderbird Creek below.

Distance: 2.0 miles out and back

Approximate hiking time: 1 to 2 hours

Difficulty: Easy

Elevation gain: 338 feet

Trail surface: Dirt and stone path

Best season: Summer through fall; open year-round

Other trail users: None

Canine compatibility: Leashed dogs permitted

Fees and permits: No fees or permits required

Maps: USGS Anchorage; Imus Geographics Chugach State Park map (www.imusgeographics.com)

Trail contacts: Chugach State Park Headquarters, Potter Section House State Historic Site, Mile 115 Seward Highway (mailing address: 18620 Seward Highway, Anchorage 99516); (907) 345-5014; http://dnr.alaska.gov/parks/index.htm; e-mail: dnr.pic@alaska.gov. Park headquarters is open Monday through Friday 10 a.m. to 4:30 p.m.

Special considerations: This trail has extremely steep and dangerous banks. Stay on the trail.

Finding the trailhead: From Anchorage follow the Glenn Highway north for 25 miles to the Thunderbird Falls exit. Veer right and continue for 0.25 mile. The well-developed parking lot on the right-hand side of the road has restroom facilities and picnic tables. GPS: N61 26.946 / W149 22.223

The Hike

The trail to Thunderbird Falls is wide, relatively straight, and easy to follow. The scenery is particularly enjoyable as you walk through a mixed spruce-hardwood forest. The path traverses the hillside with ups and downs as you proceed along the trail. The right side of the trail is occupied by private property and homes; directly on the left side is a deep gorge

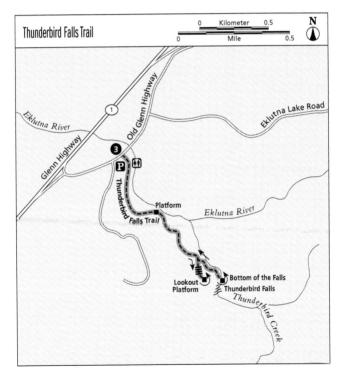

revealing the Eklutna River and eventually Thunderbird Creek.

After approximately half a mile, you reach a viewing platform that looks out toward West and East Twin Peaks and down on the glacial-silt-infused water of the Eklutna River. Continuing on the path, come to a fork where the trail turns abruptly to your left, downhill. Continue straight on the Thunderbird Trail, which joins a boardwalk. The trail ends at the second viewing deck with an unobstructed view of the falls.

The fork to the left heads steeply downhill into the gorge and Thunderbird Creek. This portion of the trail can be particularly muddy at the bottom but is worth exploring if you have the time and energy. Proceeding along the creek, you will arrive at a viewing deck near the bottom of the falls. The trail ends here. The view of the falls is not unobstructed from the bottom, but the hike down is still worth it just to observe the beauty of the huge boulders and rock-lined creek. To help in erosion control, when heading back up, stay on the main trail rather than taking the unofficial shortcuts.

This trail is popular throughout the year. It is a great summer day hike, extremely beautiful in the fall, and equally scenic in winter when the falls freeze, often creating amazing ice sculptures at the foot of the falls.

Miles and Directions

0.0 Start at the trailhead at the edge of the parking lot.

0.5 Reach the first viewing platform with a view of Eklutna River.

0.85 The trail continues straight ahead on a boardwalk. (Option: Take the left-hand trail down to Thunderbird Creek and the fenced viewing area near the bottom of the falls for an additional 0.5-mile round-trip.)

1.0 Reach the end of the trail and the second viewing platform with a view of Thunderbird Falls.

2.0 Arrive back at the parking lot.

4 Albert Loop Trail

This easy, relatively flat trail is an excellent hike for the entire family, with amazing scenery, boardwalks, and viewing platforms. The trail descends down along the Eagle River and provides outstanding mountain views, wildflowers, lush vegetation, numerous areas of beaver activity, and ample opportunities for spotting wildlife.

Distance: 3.2-mile loop

Approximate hiking time: 1.5 to 2 hours

Difficulty: Easy

Elevation gain: Negligible

Trail surface: Flat, smooth terrain; pavement, gravel and dirt; several boardwalks; muddy and wet in some areas

Best season: June through August

Other trail users: Equestrians

Canine compatibility: Leashed dogs permitted

Fees and permits: Daily parking fee at the nature center's private parking lot; state park parking passes do not apply

Maps: USGS Anchorage; Imus Geographics Chugach State Park map (www.imusgeographics. com); Eagle River Nature Center map, available at the center

Trail contacts: Eagle River Nature Center, 32750 Eagle River Road, Eagle River 99577; (907) 694-2108, www.ernc.org

Special considerations: Portions of this trail are often closed August through November to allow bears undisturbed salmon fishing in the river. There have been reported bear attacks in this area.

Finding the trailhead: From Anchorage follow the Glenn Highway north toward the town of Eagle River. After 10 miles veer right onto the Hiland Road / Eagle River Loop exit. Turn right onto Eagle River Loop Road and continue for 2.5 miles. Turn right at the Lighthouse Church onto Eagle River Road and drive 10 miles to the Eagle River Nature Center parking lot. Hike 0.5 mile down the trail directly behind the nature center. The Albert Loop Trail begins at the signpost. GPS: N61 14.046 / W149 16.2589

The Hike

This is one of several great trails at Eagle River Nature Center, just 10 miles outside of the town of Eagle River.

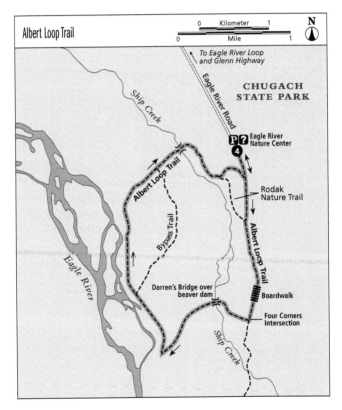

The nature center is a nonprofit organization that offers community events, public programs, and educational school programs throughout the year. They also offer guided family hikes and daily nature hikes during the summer months. Inside the center is an amazing display of local wildlife and a wealth of information about the area. Start your journey here.

The easy 3.2-mile loop provides great views of the Eagle River Valley and Polar Bear, Eagle, and Hurdygurdy Peaks. It is a fun hike with wildlife viewing opportunities, wildflowers, boardwalks, bridges, and lush vegetation.

Begin this hike just behind the nature center and proceed down the paved path on the Rodak Nature Trail. This is a popular stretch linking four trails, so plan on lots of company. However, it is closed to bicycles, motor vehicles, and horses (except by special-use permit).

Technically, the trail does not begin until you meet the junction of Dew Mound Trail and the Historic Iditarod (Crow Pass) Trail at slightly less than 0.5 mile from the trailhead. At this point the Albert Loop Trail begins by continuing straight ahead while simultaneously following the Historic Iditarod (Crow Pass) Trail. A left turn is where you begin the Dew Mound Trail. Here the ground becomes wetter, and you cross your first boardwalk to get through the wetland.

Hike another 0.5 mile to an intersection called Four Corners, for good reason. This is a prominent intersection with a resting bench. The Iditarod continues straight ahead, a left turn loops you to the Dew Mound Trail, and a right turn is the continuation of Albert Loop, which is what you want to take.

Continue onto Darren's Bridge and stop and view the large, open, marshy area on your left. This is a beautiful setting, with an abandoned beaver lodge and remnants of the beaver dam that helped form this area. Continue a short distance to reach another signpost. This gives you an opportunity to visit the River Trail Yurt, one of three yurts in the area. This one, located on the shoreline of the Eagle River, is often used by rafters and kayakers as an overnight resting facility while they travel downstream. It is also a favorite rental location for families and couples. Albert Loop continues to the right.

Farther up the trail, you will find a well-marked bypass trail veering to the right. This is often used when the river is high or during the muddy season to avoid the lower wet areas near the river. If mud is not a concern for you, take the entire trail that borders along the Eagle River. This portion of the trail allows for off-trail exploring along the stone shoreline and presents some awesome views in the valley.

At approximately 2.7 miles you come to several small bridges and a rest stop. From here on, the trail becomes gravel and narrows; the vegetation changes from woodland to tall grasses just prior to meeting the Rodak Nature Trail. You can turn right and head down to the Beaver Viewing Platform or go left, which will return you to the nature center and trailhead.

The Albert Loop Trail is a great nature trail and is used most of the year, other than several months beginning in August when it is closed because of bears fishing the Eagle River. In the winter months it provides excellent snowshoeing, hiking, and cross-country skiing opportunities.

Miles and Directions

0.0 Start hiking behind the Eagle River Nature Center.

0.9 Continue straight at the Albert Loop trailhead and begin walking on a boardwalk.

1.0 Turn right at the Four Corners intersection to stay on Albert Loop.

1.2 Reach a marshy area to your left, and a boardwalk, then cross Darren's Bridge over an old beaver dam.

1.6 Veer right, or go straight if heading to the River Trail Yurt.

1.7 Turn right to stay on the trail or left to view the river.

1.9 Main trail joins the bypass trail option used during wet seasons.

2.7 Come to the first of several bridge crossings and a bench.

3.1 The Albert Loop Trail joins the Rodak Nature Trail here. Turn left to return to the nature center.

3.2 Arrive back at the trailhead.

5 Rodak Nature Trail

This popular trail is usually packed with walkers, parents with strollers, and family dogs—all easily accommodated. The wheelchair-accessible trail begins on a wide, slightly downhill path to two viewing platforms with views of beaver activity, spawning salmon, and Eagle River Valley. There are interpretive signboards, abundant wildflowers, lush vegetation, and great scenery throughout the hike.

Distance: 0.75-mile loop
Approximate hiking time: 30 minutes to 1 hour
Difficulty: Easy
Elevation gain: −51 feet (descent)
Trail surface: Paved path and gravel with seating; wheelchair- and stroller-accessible
Best season: Summer
Other trail users: None
Canine compatibility: Leashed dogs permitted

Fees and permits: Daily parking fee at the nature center's private parking lot; state park parking passes do not apply
Maps: USGS Anchorage; Imus Geographics Chugach State Park map (www.imusgeographics.com); Eagle River Nature Center map, available at the center
Trail contacts: Eagle River Nature Center, 32750 Eagle River Road, Eagle River 99577; (907) 694-2108, www.ernc.org
Special considerations: None

Finding the trailhead: From Anchorage follow the Glenn Highway north toward the town of Eagle River. After 10 miles veer right onto the Hiland Road / Eagle River Loop exit. Turn right onto Eagle River Loop Road and continue for 2.5 miles. Turn right at the Lighthouse Church onto Eagle River Road and drive 10 miles to the Eagle River Nature Center parking lot. The trailhead is located behind the nature center. GPS: N61 14.043 / W149 16.262

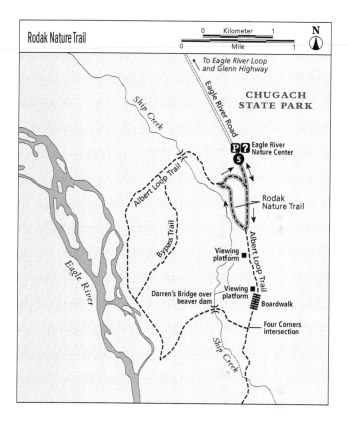

0   Kilometer   1

0   Mile   1

N

To Eagle River Loop
and Glenn Highway

CHUGACH
STATE PARK

Ship Creek

Eagle River Road

P ? Eagle River
Nature Center
5

Rodak
Nature Trail

Albert Loop Trail

Bypass Trail

Eagle River

Albert Loop Trail

Viewing
platform

Darren's Bridge over
beaver dam

Viewing
platform

Boardwalk

Four Corners
intersection

Ship Creek

The Hike

The Rodak Nature Trail is as popular with local residents as
it is with tourists. It provides a quick, easy hike for the entire
family on a nice weekend or on an evening when you want
to take a leisurely walk and enjoy nature. Before starting out
on the trail, take a few moments to visit the nature center.
The center and staff can provide a wealth of information
about the area, including its history, natural history, Alaska's

flora and fauna, and things to see and recent sightings along the trail.

To reach the nature trail, walk around to the back of the center; the trailhead is located to the left side of the patio and viewing area. A series of interpretive panels along the trail highlight many of the features of Eagle River Valley. In addition, there is always something to see along the trail as you make your way down to the river.

Trek through deciduous-coniferous woodland where an abundance of spring and summer wildflowers attractively garnish the trail's edge. The trail passes two separate viewing decks. In late August and early September the river becomes heavily populated with red and silver salmon, which are easily viewed from both platforms. Obvious evidence of beaver activity and other nocturnal wildlife are apparent along the water's edge.

Both viewing platforms provide extraordinary views of the mountain ranges and Eagle River Valley. This exceptionally beautiful area shouldn't be missed.

Miles and Directions

0.0 Start at the trailhead located directly behind the Eagle River Nature Center and turn right onto the Rodak Nature Trail. (Option: Go straight to access the Albert Loop, Historic Iditarod [Crow Pass], and Dew Mound Trails.)

0.1 Veer left at the Geology Tour #3 interpretive panel.

0.2 Reach the first viewing platform.

0.3 Reach the second viewing platform and the boardwalk.

0.4 Join the main trail. Turn left to head back to the nature center and trailhead.

0.75 Arrive back at the trailhead.

6 Dew Mound Trail

Dew Mound Trail runs parallel to the Historic Iditarod (Crow Pass) Trail. Although it is considered a one-way trail to Dew Lake, it is easily traveled as a loop along the Iditarod Trail back to the Eagle River Nature Center. This easy to moderate 6.3-mile loop trail offers four cut-back options along the way to shorten the hike, should you decide to head back sooner. The trail passes through a variety of plant communities showcasing tall grasses, shrubs and thickets, and beautiful spans of spruce, birch, and aspen trees. Large boulder fields and rocky ravines add to the adventure of this hike, along with the occasional moose or bear sighting.

Distance: 6.3-mile loop
Approximate hiking time: 3 to 4 hours
Difficulty: Easy to moderate
Elevation gain: 365 feet
Trail surface: Dirt, wood chips, tree roots, rocks and gravel
Best season: Spring, summer, fall
Other trail users: None
Canine compatibility: Leashed dogs permitted
Fees and permits: Daily parking fee in the nature center's private parking lot; state park parking passes not valid here.
Maps: Eagle River Nature Center map (available at the center);

Imus Geographics Chugach State Park map (www.imusgeographics. com); USGS Anchorage
Trail contacts: Eagle River Nature Center, 32750 Eagle River Road, Eagle River 99577; (907) 694-2108; www.ernc.org. Open Tuesday through Sunday, 10 a.m. to 5 p.m., June through August; Wednesday through Sunday, 10 a.m. to 5 p.m., May and September; Friday through Sunday, 10 a.m. to 5 p.m., October through April.
Special considerations: None

Finding the trailhead: Coming from Anchorage, follow the Glenn Highway north toward the town of Eagle River. After about 10 miles veer right onto the Hiland Road / Eagle River Loop exit. Turn right onto Eagle River Loop Road and continue for 2.5 miles. Turn right at the Walmart onto Eagle River Road and drive 10 miles to the Eagle River Nature Center parking lot. The trailhead is located behind the nature center. GPS: N61 14.045 / W149 16.260

The Hike

Begin this hike at the trailhead located behind the Eagle River Nature Center. Head straight down the Albert Loop Trail, following the gravel path. Hike about 0.4 mile and pick up Dew Mound Trail on your left. Proceeding straight will keep you on the Historic Iditarod (Crow Pass) and Albert Loop Trails; turning right will take you to the viewing deck on the Rodak Nature Trail. The trail begins through an open, grassy meadow and eventually takes you into thicker vegetation and then into a mature forest of birch, aspen, and cottonwood trees. Portions of the trail are rough with rocks and roots.

Within another 0.1 mile, come to an area with a couple of right-turn options within 15 yards of each other. Either turn will loop back to the main trail and back to the nature center. As you continue straight ahead, notice the orange blazes marking the trail. Several areas along the path are more difficult to follow, and you'll be glad you have the blazes. During the next 0.75 mile you will cross three footbridges and mountain streams, all showcasing the beauty of this area with stands of birch and spruce. Just past the third bridge you have a second opportunity to loop back to the Iditarod Trail, which will also lead you back to the nature center. The loop is called the Mountain Meadow Trail. There is one last

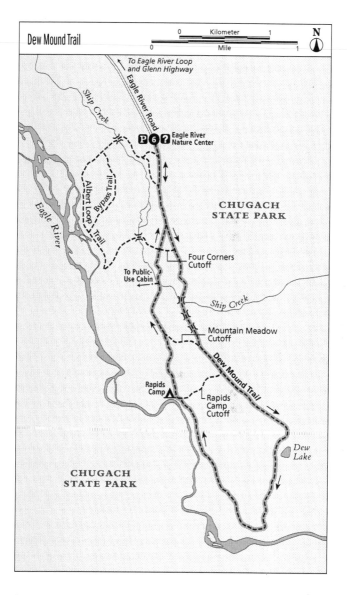

Dew Mound Trail

0   Kilometer   1

0   Mile   1

N

To Eagle River Loop and Glenn Highway

Eagle River Road

Ship Creek

P 6 ? Eagle River Nature Center

CHUGACH STATE PARK

Albert Loop Trail

Bypass Trail

Eagle River

Four Corners Cutoff

To Public- Use Cabin

Ship Creek

Mountain Meadow Cutoff

Dew Mound Trail

Rapids Camp

Rapids Camp Cutoff

Dew Lake

CHUGACH STATE PARK

opportunity to loop back another 0.25 mile up the trail. Turn right to take the Rapids Loop Trail back to the nature center and shorten the hike, or continue straight ahead to stay on the Dew Mound Trail.

The terrain begins to change rapidly with a steeper climb, rocks, and large boulders, which all add to the beauty of this hike. Once you start in the rocky terrain, within 0.5 mile you'll have a small, unbridged stream to cross. You are more likely to get wet feet from the mud than from crossing the stream. After crossing the stream, the trail heads uphill and veers to the right. Be sure to follow the orange blazes in this area. There are several places with some great scenic views from atop the rocks when you venture slightly off the trail. The trail begins to descend, passes a small pond, and within another 0.5 mile joins the Iditarod Trail down at the Eagle River. There is a small designated campsite called Echo Bend right along the river's shoreline. Be sure to use the provided metal fire ring for any campfires.

Just about where the campsite is located, Dew Mound Trail heads back north toward the nature center following the Iditarod Trail. It is a 3.2-mile hike back to the trailhead from this point. The trail is very rocky and rough from here on for about 2.0 miles. After about 1.25 miles you will arrive at another point where there is access to the Eagle River. Turn left to descend a steep series of wooden stairs and view the river. An immediate right at the signpost will take you to the Rapids Camp Yurt, which overlooks the river below. Keep in mind that the yurt might be occupied. (Advance reservations are required.) Like with most of the cabins and yurts in the park, firewood, a wood-burning stove, and bunks are provided. As you continue back toward the nature center, remember that the several trails you will be passing on your right are the same optional loop trails you passed when you were heading south on Dew Mound.

Just under 1.0 mile from the Rapids Camp, you'll come to the Paradise Haven public-use cabin signpost. This rustic log cabin, located west of the trail, is quite popular and is rented most of the time. The next intersection is called Four Corners. Turn left if you want to hike the Albert Loop Trail, which will also end up back at the nature center. Otherwise, continue straight ahead. Follow a long, narrow boardwalk over the wetland area and begin a slight uphill walk back to the center.

Miles and Directions

0.0 Start behind the Eagle River Nature Center and go straight on the Albert Loop Trail.

0.4 Turn left onto Dew Mound Trail. (Options: Straight ahead takes you onto the Historic Iditarod [Crow Pass] Trail. A right turn takes you to a viewing deck on the Rodak Nature Trail.)

0.5 Keep straight to remain on the Dew Mound Trail. (Option: Turn right to take the Four Corners Cutoff Trail back to the Iditarod Trail or back to the nature center.)

0.8 Arrive at the first footbridge. of three short boardwalks.

1.3 Continue straight on the Dew Mound Trail. (Option: Turn right to take the Mountain Meadow Cutoff Trail back to the Iditarod Trail or back to the nature center.)

1.5 Continue straight on the Dew Mound Trail. (Option: Turn right to take the Rapids Cutoff Trail back to the Iditarod Trail or back to the nature center.)

1.6 Pass large boulders on the trail.

2.25 Cross a small stream and continue straight to Dew Lake.

2.3 Backtrack and veer to the right, up a steep hill, and follow the orange blazes.

2.4 Veer slightly right onto a side trail to Dew Mound for views of the valley.

3.1 Join the Iditarod Trail at the Eagle River.

3.2 Reach the Echo Bend campsite with fire ring along the riverside.

4.3 Come to the Rapids Camp river access, then go straight at the signpost to return to the nature center. (Option: Turn right to visit the Rapids Camp Yurt.)

4.9 The Mountain Meadow Cutoff Trail to the right connects to the first leg of the Dew Mound Trail. Stay straight.

5.3 Reach the signpost for the Paradise Haven public-use cabin.

5.8 Continue straight at the Four Corners intersection.

6.0 Cross wetlands on a long, narrow boardwalk.

6.3 Arrive back at the nature center.

7 Mount Baldy Trail

This popular family trail starts out on a gravel road that heads uphill and then levels out to travel through a segment of thick alders before climbing above the tree line. The easy-to-follow trail provides good views of the town of Eagle River and Eagle River Valley. The trail is steep, has some loose stone, and can be slick when wet, but it's still a fun trail for the entire family, including the family pet.

Distance: 2.0 miles out and back
Approximate hiking time: 2 to 3 hours
Difficulty: Easy to moderate due to steepness
Elevation gain: 1,173 feet
Trail surface: Gravel, dirt, stone
Best season: May through September
Other trail users: Runners
Canine compatibility: Leashed dogs permitted
Fees and permits: No fees or permits required

Maps: USGS Anchorage; Imus Geographics Chugach State Park map (www.imusgeographics.com)
Trail contacts: Chugach State Park Headquarters, Potter Section House State Historic Site, Mile 115 Seward Highway (mailing address: 18620 Seward Highway, Anchorage 99516); (907) 345-5014; http://dnr.alaska.gov/parks/index.htm; e-mail: dnr.pic@alaska.gov. Park headquarters is open Monday through Friday 10 a.m. to 4:30 p.m.
Special considerations: Slick when wet

Finding the trailhead: From Anchorage drive north approximately 10 miles on the Glenn Highway to the Hiland Road / Eagle River Loop exit. Exit to the right and follow Eagle River Loop Road down the hill and across the Eagle River. Pass Walmart on the right. Go through the light and the intersection of Eagle River and Eagle River Loop Roads and continue straight for several more blocks. Turn right onto Skyview Drive, which will change names a couple of times. Stay on the main road and follow it approximately 2 miles to the end. Parking is limited and is roadside only. GPS: N61 20.280 / W149 30.730

The Hike

Mount Baldy is so named because of its prominently displayed bald, rocky top. The trail begins on a gravel road that starts out abruptly uphill, then levels out and switches back toward a series of TV towers. Turn off to your left just 20 or 30 feet prior to reaching the red gate. If you continue through the gate, the gravel road will take you to the radio towers and eventually back down to the road you drove in on.

After turning left down the narrow dirt path, hike through thick stands of alders, willows, and small trees. The path begins a slight ascent toward Mount Baldy. After approximately half a mile, you come to a level area where the vegetation begins to thin and you find yourself moving above the tree line.

From here the trail becomes noticeably steeper. Use caution when trail conditions are wet, as the path can become quite slick. The trail surface becomes a mix of dirt, loose stone, and rock as you get closer to the summit. The views from the top are great, and there is plenty of wide-open space and opportunity to continue exploring the surrounding peaks. Use caution as you descend back to the gravel road.

Miles and Directions

0.0 Start at the end of the road and head uphill on a gravel road.

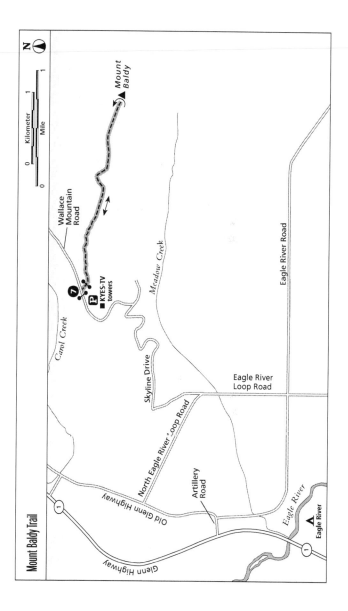

Mount Baldy Trail

0.2 Turn left and slightly downhill just before reaching a gate.

0.6 Come to a flat area before starting a steep ascent.

1.0 Arrive at the top of Mount Baldy. Enjoy the views or do a little exploring before carefully retracing your steps.

2.0 Arrive back at the parking area.

8 Rendezvous Peak Trail

The trail to Rendezvous Peak presents some of the best
views of Anchorage and the Eagle River Valley. At nearly
4,100 feet and approximately a 1,300-foot elevation gain,
you can view the Cook Inlet, Knik Arm, the Anchorage
Bowl, Mount Susitna, Fire Island, Eagle River Valley, and
Ship Creek. The trail starts out easy and becomes a bit more
difficult as you ascend the peak. Wildlife is evident, including
Arctic ground squirrels, moose, and bears, along with wildflowers and seasonal berry picking.

Distance: 3.2-mile loop
Approximate hiking time: 3 to
4 hours
Difficulty: Easy starting out,
moderate while ascending peak
Elevation gain: 1,354 feet
Trail Surface: Dirt and stone
Best season: June through
August
Other trail users: Runners
Canine compatibility: Leashed
dogs permitted

Fees and permits: Daily parking
fee. The trailhead is maintained
by the Anchorage Ski Club.
Maps: National Geographic,
Alaska, Chugach State Park
Anchorage, Trails Illustrated Topo-
graphical Map
Trail contacts: Chugach State
Park, Arctic Valley Ski Club
Special considerations: Military
land; please respect the bound-
aries

Finding the Trailhead: The Arctic Valley trailhead is at the end of
Arctic Valley Road. Coming from Anchorage, take the Glenn Highway
to the Arctic Valley exit. This road will become gravel after 2 to 3
miles. Follow this for approximately 8 miles to the parking area run
by the Anchorage Ski Club. There is a daily parking fee payable at
the fee station, where you will also find the trailhead. Your state park

or military parking pass is not valid here. GPS: N61 14.815 / W149 32.103

Note: This trail is also accessible from Eagle River. Take the Glenn Highway from Anchorage to the Hiland Road / Eagle River Loop exit. Turn right off the highway, and then take another right onto Hiland Road. Follow about 7 miles to the end. Turn right on South Creek Road, and then take another right onto West Creek Drive. The parking area for the trailhead will be on your left. There is no parking fee at this location.

The Hike

The trail information here describes hiking from the Arctic Valley side. Several miles prior to the trailhead you will drive on a gravel road. Driving slowly on this very rough road can save some unnecessary wear on your vehicle. You will be driving through and hiking near military land, so respect all signs. You will also notice military installation signs on the land. These are restricted areas, and access is prohibited. Also note that the road is gated, and is open from 6 a.m. to 10 p.m., so plan your hike accordingly. The old Nike missile site is visible from the trail, but is also on restricted land.

The official trailhead is located at the kiosk and fee station. The hike can be started here, or through the gate, to the left of the ski lodge building. The trail by the building is wide and well-traveled, and proceeds slightly uphill.

From the official trailhead start, you will see a small signpost with two signs featuring arrows pointing up the trail, behind the kiosk. One reads Rendezvous Peak Trail, and the other reads South Fork Overlook. Hike about 200 feet in the direction the sign is pointing and look for a second, narrower dirt trail off to your right. There is no sign at this turning point. Turn right and follow the meandering foot trail about

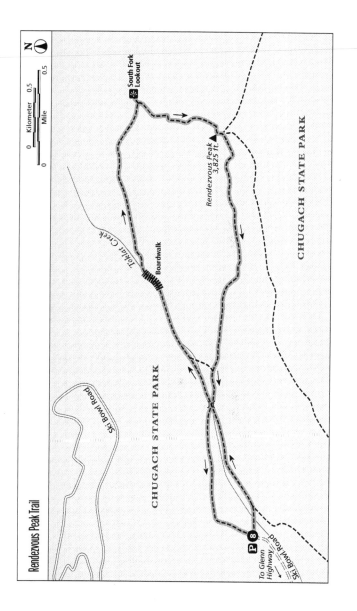

Rendezvous Peak Trail

0.25 mile to a bridge that crosses the Toklat Creek. Rather than crossing the bridge, continue straight ahead on the path. If you start your hike coming from the wide trail passing the lodge, you would cross this bridge and continue ahead on this same trail.

Travel this path slightly uphill for about half a mile. You will come to a ridgeline at the South Fork Lookout with beautiful views of the valley below. Going left will take you to Mount Gordon Lyons. Turning right will take you up to Rendezvous Peak.

You will traverse another half-mile along the saddle. The trail will go steeply uphill as it wraps around the peak and brings you to the summit. Continue on the trail while still wrapping around the peak to head back down the mountain, looping back to the trailhead and parking lot.

Miles and Directions

0.0 Start at the trailhead and pay station.

0.1 Pass through the gate.

0.4 Cross over bridge and Toklat Creek.

0.6 Cross small bridge.

0.8 Cross over short boardwalk.

1.5 View of South Fork Eagle River below.

1.9 Arrive at top of peak.

2.8 Turn right at fork and cross bridge to continue return loop.

3.1 Turn left to return to main trail and trailhead.

3.2 Arrive back at trailhead.

Hillside Trail System

A ccess to the western trails in Chugach State Park is gained from the hillside of east Anchorage. Four major trailheads access the assortment of trails called the Hillside Trail System. The trails range from easy, wide old roadbeds to more difficult routes requiring hiking experience and mountaineering skills. Excellent alpine scenery and lakes, wildflowers, fall berry picking, wildlife, and outstanding views of Anchorage, the Alaska Mountain Range, and Cook Inlet are some of the highlights on the trails.

The trails form a network that enables them to be accessed from various points on the hillside. Residents and visitors alike use the trails year-round for hiking, running, and mountain biking. The trails are heavily used in summer and fall and equally popular in winter with skiers and snow machine riders.

This area of the park has something for everyone, and the four system trails provided in this guide are but a sample. For more Hillside Trail System hikes, see *Best Hikes Anchorage: The Greatest Views, Wildlife, and Forest Strolls.*

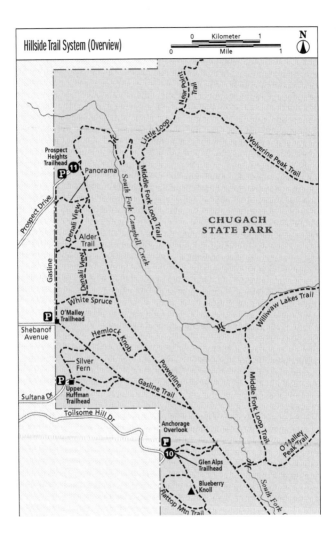

Hillside Trail System (Overview)

Kilometer
0   1
Mile
0   1

N

Prospect Heights Trailhead

Panorama

Prospect Drive

Gasline

Denali View

Alder Trail

Denali View

White Spruce

O'Malley Trailhead

Shebanof Avenue

Silver Fern

Upper Huffman Trailhead

Sultana Dr

Toilsome Hill Dr

Near Point Trail

Little Loop

South Fork Campbell Creek

Middle Fork Loop Trail

Wolverine Peak Trail

CHUGACH STATE PARK

Williwaw Lakes Trail

Hemlock Knob

Powerline

Gasline Trail

Middle Fork Loop Trail

Anchorage Overlook

Glen Alps Trailhead

Blueberry Knoll

Flattop Mtn Trail

O'Malley Peak Trail

South Fork

11

10

9 Flattop Mountain Trail

Flattop Mountain is the most climbed peak in all of Alaska, so plan on plenty of company on this trail. Although slightly more difficult than many hikes in this guide, the well-maintained trail is short in duration and easily accomplished in a few hours. Don't let the difficulty rating discourage you. A little extra effort to Flattop plateau will gain you extraordinary views of the Alaska Range, Turnagain Arm, Cook Inlet, and Anchorage—and a high point of 3,550 feet. There is an alternate route that takes you to the plateau going up the backside of the mountain. It is composed of a series of switchbacks, eliminating the scrambling to reach the top.

Distance: 2.0 miles out and back; 3.1 miles out and back to the plateau

Approximate hiking time: 3 to 5 hours for complete trail

Difficulty: Moderate; challenging for optional climb to the plateau due to steep trail and scrambling

Elevation gain: 1,300 feet to top

Trail surface: Gravel and rock

Best season: Summer and fall, although hiked year-round

Other trail users: None

Canine compatibility: Leashed dogs permitted but not recommended

Fees and permits: Parking fee at Glen Alps trailhead

Maps: USGS Anchorage; Imus Geographics Chugach State Park map (www.imusgeographics.com); Alaska Department of Natural Resources: Chugach State Park Hillside Trail System map

Trail contacts: Chugach State Park Headquarters, Potter Section House State Historic Site, Mile 115 Seward Highway (mailing address: 18620 Seward Highway, Anchorage 99516); (907) 345-5014; http://dnr.alaska.gov/parks/index.htm; e-mail: dnr.pic@alaska.gov. Park headquarters is open Monday through Friday 10 a.m. to 4:30 p.m.

Special considerations: Some areas of the trail are rough and steep with loose rock.

Finding the trailhead: From downtown Anchorage drive south on the Seward Highway to the O'Malley Road exit. Turn left (east) onto O'Malley Road and drive toward the mountains for 3.5 miles. Turn right (south) onto Hillside Drive and continue approximately 1 mile. Turn left at the sign for Upper Huffman Road. Travel 0.75 mile to an intersection where you will see a sign for Chugach State Park. Turn right onto Toilsome Hill Drive and continue for about 2 miles as the road winds and climbs and eventually becomes gravel. The Glen Alps trailhead is located on your left. The sizable parking area is equipped with a viewing deck and restroom facilities. The trail begins at the east end of the parking lot at the wooden stairs. GPS: N61 06.181 / W149 40.993

The Hike

Begin the hike by climbing the wooden stairs. The stairway quickly ends, and you follow a winding gravel trail through a brushy hemlock and spruce area. After about half a mile, you'll come to a flat, open plateau with a good view of the city of Anchorage. Wildflowers are conspicuous in spring, summer, and fall throughout this area. Just beyond this clearing is the base of Blueberry Hill, with an information board and resting bench. You have an option at this intersection to turn right and continue on the trail or to follow a loop back to the parking lot.

Stay on the trail and arrive at an area where the trail is bordered by a chain-link fence. This is an effort to help control erosion and keep the high level of traffic on the main path. Just beyond the end of the fence is an intersection.

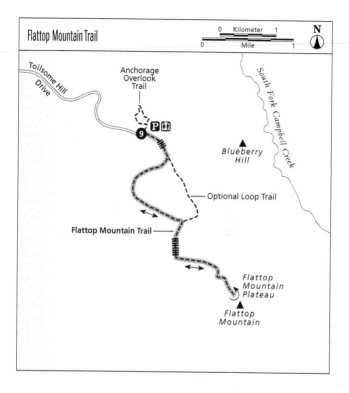

Flattop Mountain Trail

The trail turns right at this point. Going straight ahead will loop back to the parking lot. You can see where the old foot trail—no longer maintained or in use—converges at this point. Turn right to reach a series of wooden steps that climb the side of the mountain. At the top of the steps is a wooden bench, which serves as a good resting spot. This is also a phenomenal place for photo opportunities. If you're not up for the climb ahead, this is a good turnaround spot.

For the more adventurous, continue on. From this point on the scrambling begins. After 1.25 miles you will come to a sign that states young children and pets are not recommended beyond this point. The trail becomes increasingly more difficult. The rocks are flagged in yellow to help you stay on the trail. There is generally no shortage of other hikers on this trail, and you shouldn't have any problem navigating your way up the mountain. Be prepared, however, to use both hands for balance and climbing. Many hikers use gloves on this hike and collapse their hiking sticks as they climb the rocks.

As you continue your climb, watch for falling rocks that have been dislodged by hikers above you. Also be careful of rocks you dislodge that might hit hikers below. Be sure to shout out a warning if this happens. When you reach the summit plateau of Flattop, don't be surprised if it is quite windy. You should be able to observe wildflowers, lichens, and Arctic ground squirrels, along with great views of the Anchorage Bowl, Cook Inlet, Denali, and the Alaska Range.

Miles and Directions

0.0 Start at the wooden stairway at the east end of the parking lot. After 500 feet you will reach a clear flat area with a great view of Anchorage.

0.2 Arrive at the base of Blueberry Hill, where there is an information board and bench.

0.7 A chain-link fence borders the path.

0.8 Turn right at the trail junction and head toward the second saddle.

0.9 Wooden steps begin.

1.0 Reach a resting bench with a scenic view. If you're hiking with small children or not up to the climb ahead, turn around here for a moderate 2.0-mile out-and-back hike.

2.0 Arrive back at the wooden stairs and parking lot.

Optional climb to the Flattop plateau: The following mile-points continue from Milepoint 1.0 above.

1.25 Come to a trail post. The trail becomes increasingly rough and rocky.

1.55 Reach the top of Flattop and end of the trail. Enjoy the views, and after a well-deserved rest, retrace your path to the trailhead. (Option: Instead of totally retracing your steps, take the loop trail back from the summit. The loop rejoins the main trail at Blueberry Hill in just under 0.5 mile.)

3.1 Arrive back at the wooden stairs and parking lot.

10 Backside of Flattop Mountain Trail

The Backside of Flattop Mountain is the newer of the two access points constructed by Alaska State Parks for reaching the popular Flattop Mountain destination. This option trail consists of a series of switchbacks that traverse to the summit, making it a much easier hike than hiking the traditional front side of the mountain. Parking is limited to a very small parking lot and roadside parking. Great views of Anchorage, wildflowers, and amazing scenery are part of this hike to the famous Flattop Mountain peak.

Distance: 3.6 miles out and back
Approximate hiking time: 2 to 3 hours
Difficulty: Moderate
Elevation gain: 1,607 feet
Trail surface: Dirt, gravel
Best season: April through September
Other trail users: Runners, lots of other people
Canine compatibility: Leashed dogs permitted
Fees and permits: Daily parking fee
Maps: Imus Geographics Chugach State Park map (www.imusgeographics.com); Alaska Department of Natural Resources: Chugach State Park Hillside Trail System map; USGS Anchorage
Trail contacts: Chugach State Park Headquarters, Potter Section House State Historic Site, Mile 115 Seward Highway (mailing address: 18620 Seward Highway, Anchorage 99516); (907) 345-5014; http://dnr.alaska.gov/parks/index.htm; e-mail: dnr.pic@alaska.gov. Park headquarters is open Monday through Friday 10 a.m. to 4:30 p.m.
Special considerations: Slick when wet

Finding the trailhead: The trailhead is approximately a 30-minute drive from downtown Anchorage. Coming from downtown Anchorage, head east on 6th Avenue and turn left onto AK-1 / Gambell Street. Continue south 8.7 miles to the De Armoun Road exit. Continue east on De Armoun Road for 6.3 miles. Keep right onto Canyon Road for about 1 mile. Continue onto Upper Canyon Road for 0.6 mile. This becomes Highland Road / Canyon Road for about 0.2 mile. Destination will be on your right. GPS: N61 04.914 / W149 40.884

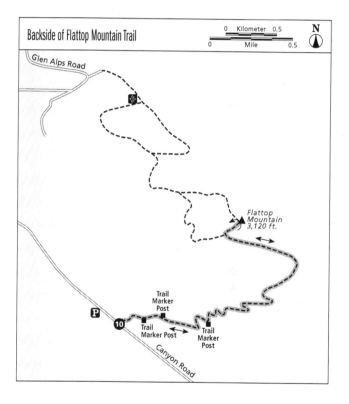

The Hike

Hiking the Backside of Flattop Mountain is a new alternative to hiking to the summit of the most widely hiked mountain in the state of Alaska.

Begin the hike at the marked trailhead along the roadside just 100 feet away from the small parking lot. The trail begins immediately with a slight uphill climb and will continue all the way to the top.

The first trail marker post is at mile 0.2, the second one, at mile 0.3, and the third one, at mile 0.6. You will be hiking through alders the first part of the trail, and the vegetation will change to wildflowers and meadows. The trail will continue as a series of switchbacks as it slowly gains in elevation. Keep your eyes open for Dall sheep on the surrounding mountain ranges as you climb and enjoy the beautiful views of Anchorage and Turnagain Arm.

Once you hike out of the meadows and into the tundra, you are likely to hear and see Arctic ground squirrels. The hike will straighten out and take you to the backside of Flattop Mountain. Hike across the rocky flat and head toward the flag, your final destination.

Miles and Directions

0.0 Start at trailhead alongside the road.

0.2 Arrive at trail marker post.

0.3 Arrive at second trail marker post,

0.6 Arrive at third trail marker post.

1.8 End at flag on top of Flattop Mountain.

3.6 Arrive back at trailhead.

11 Powerline Trail

At first glance the Powerline Trail doesn't appear to be much more than a long dirt road connecting to Indian Valley. The first 6.0 miles of this trail are uniquely different from the last 5.0 miles in regard to terrain, vegetation, and even wildlife. Steep mountain walls, mountain peaks, beautiful valleys and streams, mature Sitka spruce forest, and areas rich in wildlife provide plenty of enjoyment along the way. The trail is generally wide and uphill until it reaches the pass and then becomes very steep as it heads down to Indian Valley. This year-round multiuse trail provides access to other trails in the Hillside Trail System.

Distance: 11.3 miles one-way to Indian trailhead; 12.0 miles out and back to top of pass from Glen Alps trailhead; 10.3 miles out and back to top of pass from Indian trailhead

Approximate hiking time: 8 to 10 hours out and back from Glen Alps; 6 to 8 hours out and back from Indian

Difficulty: Easy to moderate due to steepness

Elevation gain/loss: 1,300 feet from Glen Alps; 1,960 feet from Indian

Trail surface: Wide road; dirt, gravel, and loose stone

Best season: June through mid-September

Other trail users: Bikers, horses, cross-country skiers

Canine compatibility: Leashed dogs permitted; under voice control after trailhead

Fees and permits: Daily parking fee at Glen Alps trailhead

Maps: Imus Geographics Chugach State Park map (www.imusgeographics.com); Alaska Department of Natural Resources: Chugach State Park Hillside Trail System map; USGS Anchorage

Trail contacts: Chugach State Park Headquarters, Potter Section House State Historic Site, Mile

115 Seward Highway (mailing address: 18620 Seward Highway, Anchorage 99516); (907) 345-5014; http://dnr.alaska.gov/parks/index.htm; e-mail: dnr.pic@alaska.gov. Park headquarters is open Monday through Friday 10 a.m. to 4:30 p.m.

Special considerations: Some areas along this trail are extremely avalanche-prone in winter.

Finding the trailhead: This trail is easily picked up from the Glen Alps trailhead. Drive south from downtown Anchorage on Seward Highway to the O'Malley Road exit. Drive east toward the mountains for 3.5 miles and turn right onto Hillside Drive. Continue for 1 mile and turn left onto Upper Huffman Road. Travel for 0.75 mile and then turn right onto Toilsome Hill Drive. You will see the Chugach State Park sign at this intersection. The road becomes gravel and continues for another 2 miles. The parking lot is located on your left. The large lot is equipped with a viewing deck—the Anchorage Lookout Trail—and restroom facilities. Follow either one of the paths at the north side of the parking lot 0.25 mile downhill to the Powerline Trail. GPS: N61 06.184 / W149 40.990

(Option: This trail can also be accessed at the south end at Indian trailhead, located at Mile 102 on the Seward Highway, south of Anchorage. Turn toward the mountains on Ocean View Road and drive 1.4 miles to the gravel parking lot and trailhead. GPS: N60 59.974 / W149 29.974)

The Hike

From Glen Alps Trailhead

Most people begin the Powerline Trail from the Glen Alps trailhead, although it can also be accessed from the Prospect Heights trailhead. From the Glen Alps trailhead, at the north end of the parking lot next to the wood stairs, follow either one of the two trails downhill. You will quickly arrive at a gravel road and the sign indicating that you are

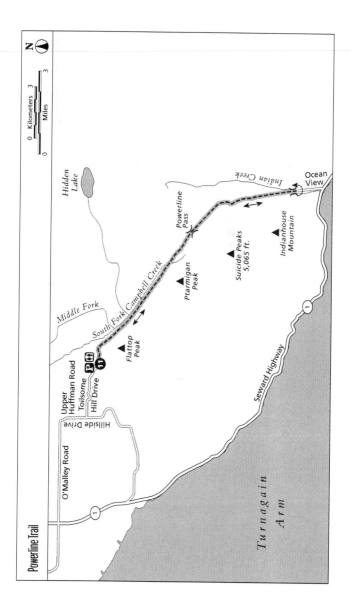

at the Powerline Trail. Immediately in front of you spanning east–west is a massive view of South Fork Campbell Creek Valley. Turn right (east). The trail heads downhill for a short distance and then begins a gradual climb for the next several miles. The path follows South Fork Campbell Creek on your left. Keep an eye out for moose along the way, both in the valley and on the trail. The trail follows the parallel power lines through the valley and over the pass. For a good day hike, travel the first 6.0 miles to the top of the pass as a 12.0-mile out-and-back hike. The last 5.0 miles look completely different and are better approached from the Indian trailhead on a separate day.

There are several turnoffs to access different trails within the Hillside Trail System along the way. Almost immediately the path to Middle Fork Loop Trail and Williwaw Lakes descends into the valley on your left. After continuing straight ahead for approximately 2.0 miles, the Hidden Lake Trailhead veers off into the valley and crosses the bridge over South Fork Campbell Creek. This trail also provides access to Ship Creek Trail.

The Powerline Trail can be very muddy and wet, with a substantial amount of mountain runoff crossing the trail. You will also encounter stream crossings at approximately 4.5 and 9.0 miles. The streams are not bridged, and you can plan on wet feet unless you bring an old pair of shoes or sandals with you.

After crossing the first stream, you soon see two small tarns on your right, the larger being Green Lake. After passing the first tarn, look for a fork to your left heading uphill and take it rather than following the wide road straight ahead that travels past the second tarn. This turnoff will take you up to the pass. If you miss it, you will quickly realize that you need to turn back to get up the steep hillside. This entire area is very avalanche-prone and begins to fill with snow by the end of September, so plan your hike accordingly. Once you are at the top of the pass, the views in both directions are amazing. Dall sheep are frequently seen at this elevation.

From here the trail heads abruptly downhill into Indian Valley. There will be a lot of rock and loose stone along the trail, making travel slightly more difficult whether you're coming up the trail or going down. Since most people will hike this trail in two parts, the hike description for the south half starts at the Indian trailhead rather than from the top of the pass.

From Indian Trailhead

For a 10.3-mile out-and-back hike from the Indian trailhead parking lot, follow the wet dirt path into the spruce forest along Indian Creek. The trail T's after approximately 0.25 mile. Turn left and cross the bridge just ahead. From here it is 4.9 miles to the pass. The path becomes muddy and wet as it begins to climb, particularly the first couple of miles. At 1.8 miles you will cross a rapidly moving stream that will most likely leave you with wet feet.

The terrain is heavily wooded and provides prime habitat for spruce grouse, bears, moose, and porcupines—the latter being good reason to keep your dog on a leash, at least through this part of the hike. As the trail continues to climb, the views of Turnagain Arm to the south and Indian Valley become increasingly amplified with the increased altitude, at around 3.0 miles. The path becomes very steep and narrow with loose stone as it travels through thick vegetation and numerous switchbacks, leaving the tree line below. As you approach the final destination, the trail surface changes to rock and stone and climbs steadily to the pass, where it over-looks the South Fork Campbell Creek Valley below.

Miles and Directions

North Section
0.0 Start at the Glen Alps trailhead parking lot.

0.25 Turn right (east) at the sign onto Powerline Trail.

0.5 Pass the Middle Fork Loop trailhead on your left; continue straight.

2.0 Pass the Hidden Lake trailhead; stay on Powerline Trail.

4.5 Cross a small, unbridged creek.

4.8 Veer left at the fork and head uphill.

6.0 Reach the top of the pass. Enjoy the views before retracing your steps. (Option: Continue down to Indian for an 11.2-mile one-way shuttle hike.)

12.0 Arrive back at the Glen Alps parking lot.

South Section
0.0 Start at the Indian trailhead parking lot.

0.25 Turn left at the T and cross a bridge (10.9 miles from Glen Alps).

0.59 Follow the fork uphill along the power lines.

1.8 Ford a rapidly moving, unbridged stream (9.0 miles from Glen Alps).

5.15 Reach the top of the pass (6.0 miles from Glen Alps). Enjoy the views before retracing your steps to the Indian parking lot. (Option: Continue down to the Glen Alps trailhead for an 11.2-mile, one-way shuttle hike.

10.3 Arrive back at the Indian trailhead parking lot.

12 Near Point Trail

If you are looking for a longer hike, this trail offers a good full-day trek to the top of a scenic ridge with truly outstanding views of the city of Anchorage. Although a little more challenging because of its length and elevation gain, this trail is worth the extra effort if you have a day to devote to one good hike. The clearly defined and well-traveled trail offers opportunities for wildlife viewing and photography, a mix of vegetative ecosystems, some great views of the Alaska Range and Cook Inlet, and an old homesite at the top of the peak.

Distance: 8.0 miles out and back

Approximate hiking time: 6 to 8 hours

Difficulty: Easy to moderate due to elevation gain

Elevation gain: 1,900 feet

Trail surface: Loose stone, mud

Best season: Summer and fall

Other trail users: Mountain bikers on first 3.0 miles

Canine compatibility: Leashed dogs permitted

Fees and permits: Parking fee at Prospect Heights trailhead

Maps: USGS Anchorage; Imus Geographics Chugach State Park map (www.imusgeographics.com); Alaska Department of Natural Resources: Chugach State Park Hillside Trail System map

Trail contacts: Chugach State Park Headquarters, Potter Section House State Historic Site, Mile 115 Seward Highway (mailing address: 18620 Seward Highway, Anchorage 99516); (907) 345-5014; http://dnr.alaska.gov/parks/index.htm; e-mail: dnr.pic@alaska.gov. Park headquarters is open Monday through Friday 10 a.m. to 4:30 p.m.

Special considerations: None

Finding the trailhead: From downtown Anchorage drive south on the Seward Highway to the O'Malley Road exit. Turn left (east) onto

O'Malley Road and drive toward the mountains for 3.5 miles. Turn right (south) onto Hillside Drive. Immediately after the road curves to the left, turn right onto Upper O'Malley Drive. Follow this road for 0.5 mile to the first intersection and turn left onto Prospect Drive. Follow Prospect Drive for another mile to the Prospect Heights trailhead. There are plenty of parking spaces and restroom facilities. The trail begins at the signboard at the northeast end of the parking lot. GPS: N61 08.332 / W149 42.692

The Hike

The trailhead is very obvious at the northeast end of the parking lot. You will also see a large signage board. It's a good idea to stop and read any notices posted by the park rangers, such as bear and bear cub sightings along the trail or precautionary notices to be aware of while hiking. Begin by following the wide trail several hundred feet to an intersection. Go left, following the power lines, with your first view of Anchorage off in the distance.

At approximately 1.0 mile, cross South Fork Campbell Creek on a well-constructed footbridge. The trail switchbacks several times before reaching another intersection. To your right is the Middle Fork Loop Trail, which eventually connects to the Glen Alps trailhead. Veer left to stay on the Near Point Trail.

Cross another stream on a small footbridge. About 1.0 mile past the bridge, a sign directs you to either Wolverine Peak or Near Point. Stay straight ahead for Near Point. (*Note:* You will often see these types of choices along the way. There are numerous other loop trail opportunities in the Hillside Trail System, and a good map would be very beneficial.)

You've been traveling mostly east up to this point and will now start heading in a more northerly direction. The

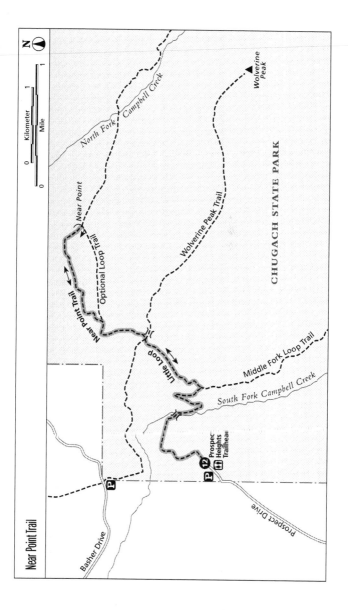

Near Point Trail

trail narrows and becomes quite steep. At approximately 3.0 miles the ground is extremely muddy and wet, and the trail may become more difficult to follow. This only lasts for several hundred feet. Just keep heading in the same direction and the path will become obvious again.

The landscape changes from forests and trees to shrubby vegetation and eventually tundra. Once you are past the muddy area, you'll be hiking on loose stone and a narrow path. As you wind your way up the mountain, the views of Anchorage below continue to be breathtaking. The ecosystem up here provides good habitat for Arctic ground squirrels and is also a popular area in the fall for wild blueberry picking.

Reach your destination at 4.0 miles and 3,050 feet elevation. A cairn has been constructed at the top of the peak, and you can observe the location of an old homesite. It can be very windy up here, so plan accordingly. Once you're there, exploring the terrain, studying the vegetation, and taking in the views will add to your enjoyment of this hike. This is a great place for lunch before you head back down.

Miles and Directions

0.0   Start at the signboard at the northeast end of the parking lot.

0.85   Cross South Fork Campbell Creek on a bridge.

1.4   Reach a trail post indicating other Hillside Trail System options. Veer left to stay on Near Point Trail.

1.55   Continue straight ahead at the trail post.

2.0   Reach a junction with the Wolverine Peak Trail on your left and right. Continue straight ahead.

2.4   The trail switches back south-southeast, affording a great view of Anchorage.

2.6 Continue on the main trail, heading north. (Option: Take the small, narrow trail on the right at the double spruce trees for an alternate loop route to the top of the plateau.)

3.0 The trail becomes extremely wet, with low vegetation.

3.6 Cross an area of tundra and loose stone.

4.0 Reach the top of the plateau. Retrace your steps back down to the trailhead.

8.0 Arrive back at the trailhead.

South of Anchorage

13 Potter Marsh Wildlife Viewing Boardwalk Trail

The Potter Marsh Wildlife Viewing Boardwalk Trail is a must-see destination for anyone interested in viewing and photographing wildlife and wild birds in south Anchorage. The 534-acre marsh is located at the south end of the Anchorage Coastal Wildlife Refuge. It is one of the most accessible and scenic wildlife viewing areas in Anchorage. Moose, black and brown bears, bald eagles, songbirds, waterfowl, shorebirds, and salmon are commonly sighted throughout the year. The boardwalk sits next to the scenic Turnagain Arm, with a beautiful mountain backdrop. Upon arrival, you will find a large paved parking area, restroom facilities, an easily traveled wooden boardwalk with benches, and several viewing platforms with spotting scopes for your use. Bring your binoculars and camera.

Distance: 1.1 miles out and back

Approximate hiking time: 1 hour

Difficulty: Easy

Elevation gain: 75 feet

Trail surface: Wooden boardwalk

Best season: Year-round

Other trail users: Birders, nature trips, school groups

Canine compatibility: No dogs allowed on boardwalk (parking lot only)

Fees and permits: No fees required

Maps: Imus Geographics, Chugach State Park Hillside Trail System: Alaska Department of Natural Resources: Chugach State Park Hillside Trail System map

Trail contacts: Alaska Department of Fish and Game, Division of Wildlife Conservation, 333 Raspberry Road, Anchorage 99518-1599; (907) 267-2189

Special considerations:
Wheelchair-friendly, good wildlife
viewing area, bathrooms on-site

Finding the trailhead: The Potter Marsh Wildlife Viewing Board-
walk Trail trailhead is conveniently located south of Anchorage on the
New Seward Highway. Coming from downtown Anchorage, head east
on 6th Avenue. Turn right onto Gambell Street and travel 4 miles.
Gambell Street will join AK-1. Continue on for 5.6 miles. Turn left
onto East 154th Avenue across from the Rabbit Creek Shooting Park.
Continue 0.3 mile to the large paved parking area. GPS: N61 04.670
/ W149 49.631

The Hike

The Potter Marsh Wildlife Viewing Boardwalk Trail begins
at the trailhead at the east side of the parking area, with an
option to travel either left or right. Turning left will take
you to an observation deck with an optional loop trail back
to the parking lot, about halfway to the end. The opposite
direction parallels the New Seward Highway and overlooks
the marsh and the Chugach Mountains. This side along the
highway can be very windy on some days, so dress accordingly. The Alaska Department of Fish and Game maintains
this site, and will generally have a volunteer host available to
answer questions during the summer months.

The site is open year-round; however, you will view different types of wildlife depending on the season. Starting in
late April running through September, Canada geese, canvas-
back ducks, red-necked phalaropes, horned and red-necked
grebes, northern pintails, and northern harriers will be found
using the marsh area. The summer months of late May
through August, when the spring and fall migrations occur,

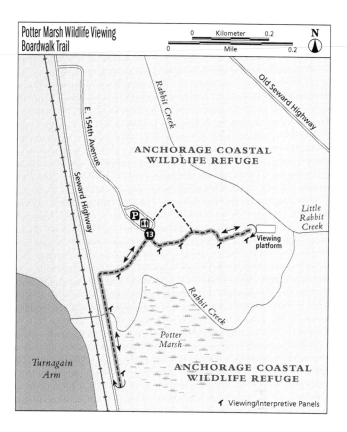

Rabbit Creek

Old Seward Highway

E. 154th Avenue

Seward Highway

**ANCHORAGE COASTAL
WILDLIFE REFUGE**

Little
Rabbit
Creek

P

13

Viewing
platform

Rabbit Creek

Potter
Marsh

Turnagain
Arm

**ANCHORAGE COASTAL
WILDLIFE REFUGE**

↑ Viewing/Interpretive Panels

gulls, arctic terns, and shorebirds are very prevalent. Trumpeter swans will also be seen.

When you walk the boardwalk to the left, toward the mountain side, you will come to Rabbit Creek, which flows directly underneath the boardwalk into the marsh. This is a good location to see several species of salmon, such as chinook, coho, and humpbacks from May to August. Continue on the boardwalk and take in the views, reading the various interpretive panels along the way and looking for other species of wildlife as you proceed to the end. Moose and an occasional bear are often seen. At the far end of the boardwalk, a pair of binoculars will help you to spot eagle nests in the tops of the large cottonwoods along the bluff. Look for their white heads up in the treetops. Continue to look for various birds and wildlife as you head back toward the trailhead, as the wildlife sightings change rapidly.

When you have finished the boardwalk, you can drive south on the New Seward Highway for about one-quarter of a mile. There is a small pull-over on the marsh side of the road. This is another good location for waterfowl viewing, nesting birds, and photography. Once again, keep your binoculars handy.

Miles and Directions

0.0 Start at the large kiosk at the trailhead in parking lot and turn left.

0.2 Arrive at end of boardwalk and large viewing platform.

0.4 Arrive back at trailhead and continue on boardwalk toward Seward Highway.

0.3 End of boardwalk along Seward Highway.

1.1 Arrive back at parking lot.

14 Turnagain Arm Trail

The historic Turnagain Arm Trail dates back to 1910, when it was used for carrying supplies during the construction of the railroad. The trail runs above and parallel to the Seward Highway, the railroad, and the beautiful waters of Turnagain Arm. It can be hiked in a day or hiked as three different segments. Throughout the trail you'll observe stands of birch, aspen, poplar, and spruce trees, highlighted by coastal vegetation, wildflowers, and numerous stream crossings. Wildlife is also abundant, ranging from spruce grouse and bears to moose and Dall sheep.

Distance: 9.3 miles one-way for entire trail (first segment, 3.5 miles; second segment, 3.8 miles; third segment, 2.0 miles)

Approximate hiking time: 6 to 8 hours for entire trail (first segment, 2 to 3 hours; second segment, 2.5 to 3 hours; third segment, 1.5 to 2 hours)

Difficulty: Easy to moderate

Elevation gain: 700 feet

Trail surface: Dirt and gravel

Best season: Summer and fall

Other trail users: None

Canine compatibility: Leashed dogs permitted at trailhead; must be under voice control on the trail

Fees and permits: Parking fee

Maps: USGS Anchorage; Imus Geographics Chugach State Park map (www.imusgeographics.com); Alaska Department of Natural Resources: Chugach State Park Hillside Trail System map

Trail contacts: Chugach State Park Headquarters, Potter Section House State Historic Site, Mile 115 Seward Highway (mailing address: 18620 Seward Highway, Anchorage 99516); (907) 345 5014; http://dnr.alaska.gov/parks/index.htm; e-mail: dnr.pic@alaska.gov. Park headquarters is open Monday through Friday 10 a.m. to 4:30 p.m.

Special considerations: None

Finding the trailhead: From Anchorage head south on the Seward Highway to Mile Marker 115. You will pass Potter Marsh on your left and the state park office on your right. The trailhead and parking are located on the left (east) side of the road, along with restroom facilities, a resting bench, and a viewing scope. The trail starts on the paved path at the overlook platform. GPS: N61 02.882 / W149 47

The Hike

This hike can easily be split into three segments and can be started from four locations: Potter Creek, McHugh, Rainbow, and Windy Corner. There are parking lots at three of the four places. Although there is room for one or two cars to park along the highway at Windy Corner, most one-way hikers arrange to be picked up here rather than leave a vehicle. The hike is numbered from north to south, beginning at the Potter Creek trailhead and ending at Windy Corner. The entire trail is well marked with signposts and mileage markers.

Begin at the overlook platform and interpretive sign display on the south side of the parking lot. Here you will find a good view of the mudflats, the railroad, and the Seward Highway below. The first 0.3 mile of this hike is part of a nature trail and has several interpretive displays along the way. The trail starts out as a paved path and then veers east into the forest and becomes a well-maintained 4-foot-wide gravel path.

You quickly come to the old Potter Road, part of a shorter loop trail, which goes straight ahead. Turn right to continue on Potter Creek Trail. After approximately half a mile, come to a T. Turn right to continue onto McHugh Creek Trail, which is the first third of the Turnagain Arm Trail. (Going left will loop you back to the old Potter Road

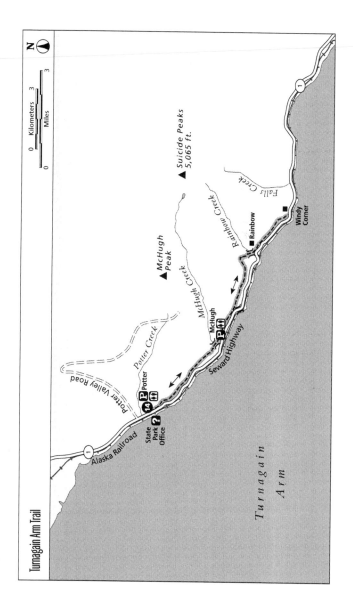

Turnagain Arm Trail

and back to the parking lot.) The trail becomes a rooted dirt path, levels off, and gets progressively rougher.

Cross a small bridge over a mountain stream at about 0.7 mile. Just beyond this stream, about another 0.1 mile, come to the first resting bench and overlook. After about 1.5 miles, cross another small bridge and stream. The trail has a tendency to be wet, and you'll encounter many small boardwalks along the way.

After about 2.2 miles, reach the junction with the 7.0-mile McHugh Lake Trail on your left. Continue straight ahead on the Turnagain Arm Trail. Slightly farther up the trail, another signpost directs you straight ahead to the next trailhead at Rainbow. (Turning right will take you to the upper-level parking lot of the McHugh Creek State Wayside at Seward Highway Mile Marker 112.)

The next trail section between McHugh and Rainbow becomes narrower, with loose stone, rock ledges, and a variety of hiking terrain. About 400 feet from the turn down to the parking lot, a second signpost directs you to make another right-hand turn. After turning, cross two more streams and bridges over the course of the next 5.0 miles. You'll have another bridgeless crossing within another mile, and you should be able to hear the water flowing down a series of small falls as you approach. At 6.0 miles the vegetation changes from birch and aspen trees to spruce. Look for spruce grouse on the trail and in the tree branches ahead. They often go unnoticed until you are practically upon them; then they suddenly take flight, startling you as you hike along the path.

The trail begins a slow descent with several switchbacks as it follows the mountain stream on your left. Just before 7.0 miles the trail crosses the stream on a bridge. Beyond the bridge the trail crosses a private drive and heads downhill toward Rainbow Creek. Rainbow is an impressive creek—fast and scenic. If you are into stream photography, this is a good one to photograph as you explore the shoreline and small falls. Cross the bridge over Rainbow Creek and follow the trail down to the Rainbow parking lot (Seward Highway Mile Marker 108), with an option to stop or continue on to Windy Corner, another 1.9 miles. You'll be able to pick up the trail to Windy Corner at the northeast corner of the lot.

On the last 2.0 miles of the trail, you can expect loose stone and a narrow path with sheer, steep ledges in places. This last segment of the trail, as you get closer to Windy, is through sheep habitat, and you may well get a glimpse of Dall sheep.

For about 1.0 mile you'll continue ascending into rocky terrain. Plan on several small stream crossings without bridges—and the possibility of wet feet. Just after Mile 9.0, keep your eye out for Dall sheep on the rocks above. This is a popular place for sheep to congregate, where they entertain the people on the Seward Highway below. The trail quickly descends to the highway below and ends at Seward Highway Mile Marker 106.

Miles and Directions

0.0 Start at the overlook platform on the paved path on the south side of the parking lot.

0.1 Veer right off old Potter Road.

0.5 Turn right at the trail post onto the McHugh Creek Trail.

0.7 Cross a small stream on a bridge.

0.8 Reach a scenic view with a bench.

1.5 Cross a bridge over a small stream.

2.2 The McHugh Lake trailhead is on your left. Continue straight ahead.

3.5 At the trail post continue straight ahead on the Turnagain Arm Trail. (Option: Turn right and travel 545 feet to the upper-level parking lot of the McHugh Creek State Wayside, Seward Highway Mile Marker 112.)

3.6 Turn right at the trail post and cross a bridge.

5.1 Reach a small stream and bridge crossing.

5.9 Reach another small stream crossing, this time with no bridge.

6.9 The trail crosses the stream on a bridge.

7.5 Cross Rainbow Creek on a bridge.

7.7 Reach the Rainbow parking lot at Seward Highway Mile Marker 108. (Option: Travel 1.9 miles to Windy Corner; pick up the trail at the northeast corner of the lot.)

8.9 Cross several small, unbridged mountain streams.

9.0 Cross another small stream at Mile Marker 9.

9.1 Reach a scenic view. Turn right off the trail to a large boulder.

9.3 Arrive at Windy Corner, Seward Highway Mile Marker 106, and pick up your shuttle.

15 Winner Creek Trail

Winner Creek Trail is a favorite for many hikers. For one thing, it is different from most every other trail in Chugach State Park and the Anchorage area. Located about 40 miles south of Anchorage, near Girdwood, the trail is actually the beginning of the northern tip of the temperate rain forest. The path goes through beautiful boreal forest composed of towering moss-covered Sitka spruce. The forest floor is also lined with moss, moss-covered decaying logs, and beautiful ferns. The highlights are two impressive gorges and a hand tram suspended by ropes and pulleys 100 feet or so above Glacier Creek. And as an added bonus—the Alyeska Resort!

Distance: 5.0 miles out and back
Approximate hiking time: 2 to 3 hours
Difficulty: Easy to moderate
Elevation gain: 400 feet
Trail surface: Pavement, dirt
Best season: Year-round
Other trail users: Walkers, runners, cyclists, skiers
Canine compatibility: Leashed dogs permitted

Fees and permits: No fees or permits required
Maps: USGS Seward; Imus Geographics Chugach State Park map (www.imusgeographics.com)
Trail contacts: Chugach National Forest, 3301 C Street, Suite 300, Anchorage 99503; (909) 743-9500; https://www.fs.usda.gov/chugach
Special considerations: None

Finding the trailhead: From Anchorage head south on the Seward Highway approximately 40 miles to Mile 90. Turn left onto the Alyeska Highway and head toward Girdwood. Travel 3 miles and turn left at the stop sign onto Arlberg Road. Follow Arlberg Road to its end at the

Alyeska Resort hotel; park in the visitor parking area at the national forest signs. GPS: N60 58.191 / W149 05.706

The Hike

Start the trail behind the Alyeska Resort hotel; the main path is obvious. On this hike, like many others in the area, be sure to pack rain gear and mosquito repellent. It can very well be sunny in downtown Anchorage with intermittent or steady light rain here. Because of the rain forest conditions, portions of the path can be wet, along with slippery boards on the trail. However, many parts of the trail are heavily graveled, making it easy traveling.

Don't let wet conditions discourage you from making this hike. This is a great scenic trail with a lot to offer, including a glimpse of Alaskan nature not seen on typical mountain trails. It is extremely well maintained and suitable for all levels of hikers.

You will immediately be amazed at the rain forest flora as you proceed up the trail from the hotel. At approximately 1.5 miles, a sign indicates you are 1.0 mile from the gorge. At about 2.1 miles the trail turns to the left. Straight ahead and slightly to the right, an old bridge crosses a creek. This is not the trail to the tram. Instead, veer to the left, following the creek.

As you approach Winner Creek Gorge, you will hear the creek well in advance. The footbridge across the deep, narrow gorge with overhanging trees is extremely impressive and dramatic, with rock formations and pounding water on the rocks below. After crossing the gorge, the trail turns left, allowing you to look back at the gorge from a different perspective. Use caution at the edges of the trail if you are trying to photograph the bridge.

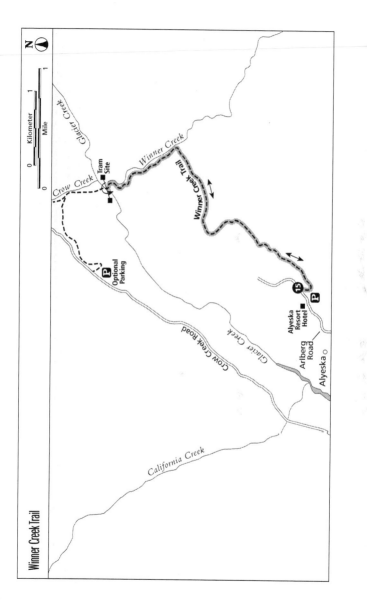

Winner Creek Trail

The hand tram is the next stop—and the final destination for most hikers. The tram consists of a steel cage that can hold two adults, and you pull your way across Glacier Creek by means of a pulley system. The crossing starts out with a slight downward dip toward the center of the creek, with gravity on your side to get you in motion. It requires some substantial effort to pull you and your partner to the other side, as the tram's path heads slightly upward. If the trail is busy that day, you will need to wait your turn for both your initial crossing and your return journey.

The trail on the other side of Glacier Creek continues for 1.0 mile and provides access to Crow Creek Mine and to a small parking lot for an alternative approach to the tram.

Miles and Directions

0.0 Start the trail behind the Alyeska Resort.

0.5 Cross a small bridge over a creek.

0.8 Cyclists must stop at this point.

1.5 Reach a sign that notes you are 1.0 mile from the tram and first gorge.

2.1 Turn left at the fork. Ignore the path that slants right to an old bridge.

2.3 Cross a footbridge over Winner Creek Gorge.

2.5 Arrive at the hand tram over Glacier Creek. This is your turn around point. (Option: Use the hand tram to cross the creek and continue 0.8 mile to the alternative parking lot on Crow Creek Road.)

5.0 Arrive back at the trailhead behind the Alyeska Resort.

Urban Anchorage Trails

16 Earthquake Park / Inside the Slide Trail

On Good Friday, March 27, 1964, an earthquake with a magnitude of 9.2 hit the Anchorage region. Lasting 4 minutes and 38 seconds, it was recorded as the largest earthquake to shake North America, and the second-most-powerful earthquake in the world. This park shows the aftereffects of that Great Alaskan Earthquake and how it permanently altered Anchorage and Southcentral Alaska. A monument and interpretive panels along the trail tell the story of this earthquake and provide some astounding facts and figures of what happened in 1964.

Within Earthquake Park is short loop dirt trail called the Slide. At the intersection of the Earthquake Park Trail and the Tony Knowles Coastal Trail, head north about 0.2 mile. Here you will find the well-marked trailhead on your right. The topography of this area shows how the land moved and was permanently altered during this historic earthquake. Both short hikes are fun and easy, and deliver some unforgettable Alaskan and national history—in addition to the occasional Anchorage moose that might be sharing the trail.

Distance: 0.75 mile out and back; Inside the Slide: 0.5-mile loop

Approximate hiking time: 45 minutes to 1 hour

Difficulty: Easy

Elevation gain: 321 feet

Trail surface: Paved, dirt

Best season: Year-round

Other trail users: Hikers, cyclists

Canine compatibility: Leashed dogs permitted

Fees and permits: No parking fees or permits required

Maps: Anchorage Trail and Parks Map: http://munimaps.muni.org/trails/reference.htm

Trail contacts: Anchorage Park Foundation, 3201 C Street, Suite 111, Anchorage 99503; (907) 274-1003; https://anchorage-parkfoundation.org/; e-mail info@anchorageparkfoundation.org

Special considerations: None

Finding the trailhead: Coming from downtown Anchorage, head west on West Fifth Avenue. Turn left onto L Street and continue onto Minnesota Drive for 1 mile. Turn right onto Northern Lights Boulevard and travel for 2.1 miles. Destination will be on your right. GPS: N61 11.780 / W149 58.653

The Hike

This is a popular stop for hikers, runners, walkers, and visitors. Upon arrival to the large paved parking lot, you will find a large visible trailhead at the far end of the lot. This short, paved, easy trail has several interpretive panels along the way and ends at a spacious open area with an exhibit and viewing deck at the water's edge of Turnagain Arm. There is a very short loop trail going around the monument that commemorates the 1964 earthquake. From there, head back out to the Tony Knowles Coastal Trail, turn left, and hike about 0.2 mile. The large open area off the paved trail to your right is the Inside the Slide trailhead.

Inside the Slide is an impressive area that was moved by the earthquake of 1964. This mass of land literally slid more than 100 feet, and the elevation was 25 to 40 feet higher after the earthquake. Within this immediate area is a series of hidden ponds and rolling hills. Be sure to follow the well-marked signs along the way, as there are numerous side trails in this area, and it's easy to get off course if you don't. The rolling and meandering trail is easy, with ten interpretive

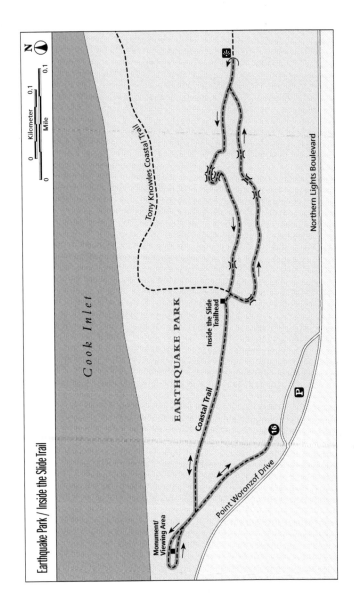

Earthquake Park / Inside the Slide Trail

Cook Inlet

EARTHQUAKE PARK

Tony Knowles Coastal Trail

Monument/
Viewing Area

Coastal Trail

Inside the Slide
Trailhead

Point Woronzof Drive

Northern Lights Boulevard

16

P

N

Kilometer

Mile

panels along the path. This area is a natural attractant for waterfowl and other types of wildlife because of the vegetation and numerous low wet areas.

Begin the trail at the trailhead. Follow the orange blazes, and be sure to make an immediate left turn that goes up a short steep hill. This immediate turn is just before a small boardwalk and a very prominent trail that continues forward. You do not want to travel on this trail beyond the bridge. If you crossed the bridge, this means you missed the turn, and the entire trail.

After going over the hill, continue onward and watch for the interpretive panels and orange trail markers throughout the hike. The trail is easy to follow at this point. You will cross a series of small bridges every several hundred feet throughout the entire trail. The series of small ponds and the wetland environment makes this trail a haven for mosquitoes, so you will want to prepare for this accordingly.

Miles and Directions

0.0 Start at Earthquake Park trailhead in parking lot.

0.3 Cross intersection of Tony Knowles Coastal Trail and follow short loop back to Coastal Trail.

0.4 Turn left onto Coastal Trail.

0.6 Arrive at Into the Slide trailhead.

0.7 Cross small bridge.

0.8 Cross another bridge.

0.9 Reach an overlook of area.

1.0 Cross another small bridge.

1.1 Cross a small bridge over wet area.

1.2 Arrive back at trailhead.

17 Lanie Fleischer Chester Creek Trail

Four main trails in the Anchorage area are considered part of the Anchorage Greenbelt: the Tony Knowles Coastal Trail, the Campbell Creek Trail, the Ship Creek Trail, and the Lanie Fleischer Chester Creek Trail, described below. This is another multipurpose trail that is heavily used throughout the year. The trail begins at the popular Westchester Lagoon and traverses toward the Chugach Mountains in the east. The easy paved path affords great scenery and a variety of wildlife-viewing opportunities along the way, as it connects many major sectors of the city.

Distance: 10.2 miles out and back
Approximate hiking time: 5 to 6 hours
Difficulty: Easy
Elevation gain: Negligible
Trail surface: Paved
Best season: Year-round
Other trail users: Walkers, runners, and cyclists; cross-country skiers in winter
Canine compatibility: Leashed dogs permitted

Fees and permits: No fees or permits required
Maps: Anchorage Trail and Parks Map: http://munimaps.muni.org/trails/reference.htm
Trail contacts: Anchorage Park Foundation, 3201 C Street, Suite 111, Anchorage 99503; (907) 274-1003; https://anchorage-parkfoundation.org/; e-mail info@anchorageparkfoundation.org
Special considerations: None

Finding the trailhead: Coming from downtown Anchorage, head south on L Street, which becomes Minnesota Drive. Turn right onto 15th Avenue; Westchester Lagoon is straight ahead. There is plenty of parking (although lots do fill up during the summer months), with two lots along the street side of the lagoon, as well as restroom facilities.

The trailhead is located on the north side of Westchester Lagoon at Margaret Eagan Sullivan Park. The trail begins at the intersection with the Tony Knowles Coastal Trail at the northwest side of the lagoon, next to a set of benches. GPS: N61 12.516 / W149 55.339

The Hike

You can expect plenty of company on any given day on the Lanie Fleischer Chester Creek Trail. It begins at the picturesque Westchester Lagoon, bordering the Knik Arm—a popular recreational area for picnicking, playing Frisbee, walking the dog, bird-watching, running, biking, and just getting out to enjoy the outdoors. Because the easterly bound trail connects to many of the parks in Anchorage, the University of Alaska and Pacific University, and medical centers along the way, it is used by many local commuters.

The trail starts at the intersection with the Tony Knowles Coastal Trail. Turn left at the intersection and head eastward along the paved path, following the shoreline of the lagoon. Veer left at the first fork and head through the tunnel that takes you under Minnesota Drive. (If you continue straight ahead, you will arrive at a parking lot and the Westchester Waterfowl Sanctuary.) Veer left again and go through another tunnel, taking you under Spenard Road. Continue for slightly less than 0.3 mile and pass under Arctic Boulevard; Valley of the Moon Park is on your right. Just before going under C Street, you will see the community gardens on your right. Pass under C Street, veer right to cross a small bridge, and immediately on your right is the small park commonly known as Gorilla Park.

At approximately 1.5 miles pass under A Street and by several access points to the Sullivan Arena on your left. The trail heads through a birch-spruce forest and crosses a bridge

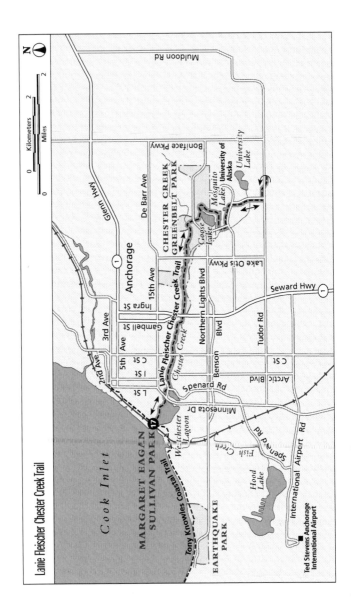
Lanie Fleischer Chester Creek Trail

at approximately 1.9 miles. At about 0.25 mile beyond the bridge, pass under the Seward Highway; then cross another bridge, pass Woodside Park, and traverse through stands of birch and spruce and a wetland area.

Follow the signs pointing toward Goose Lake. At approximately the 3.0-mile point, there's a resting bench where you can sit and appreciate the natural area and flowing waters of Chester Creek. Just beyond the rest area, arrive at a small pond on your right and then cross the creek again.

Follow the trail under the Lake Otis Parkway and pass Davenport Field. Travel another 0.5 mile and go left at the fork toward Tikishla Park. This is approximately 3.75 miles from the trailhead. Turn right just beyond the park and head over the bridge toward Goose Lake. Cross another bridge, take the fork to the right, and climb slightly uphill and over Northern Lights Boulevard. The trail T's after approximately another 0.2 mile. Turn right at this intersection. (Turning left will take you to Russian Jack Park.) Continue downhill to arrive at Goose Lake and the pavilion. Travel past the pavilion and lake and into the birch-spruce forest at a slight incline.

After approximately 0.75 mile, come to the University of Alaska parking garage and then to the intersection of Alumni Loop and UAA Drive. Turn left onto UAA Drive and then left again onto Providence Drive. The trail continues into the forest and past Mosquito Lake on your left. Cross Providence/University Drive onto Elmore Road. Follow the sidewalk, and just before reaching Tudor Road, turn left uphill to the crosswalk that will take you safely across Tudor. Follow the trail downhill, where it turns to the right and brings you to the Campbell Creek Trail trailhead.

Miles and Directions

0.0 Start in Margaret Eagan Sullivan Park at the intersection with the Tony Knowles Coastal Trail. Turn left onto the Lanie Fleischer Chester Creek Trail.

0.4 Veer left at the trail fork.

0.7 Pass under Minnesota Drive.

1.0 The trail travels under Arctic Boulevard.

1.3 Pass under C Street. The community gardens are on your right, just before the tunnel.

1.4 Cross a bridge and travel past Gorilla Park on your right.

1.5 Pass under A Street; Sullivan Arena is on your left.

1.9 Cross a bridge after walking through a birch-spruce forest.

2.2 Pass under the Seward Highway, cross a bridge, and go past Woodside Park.

3.0 Come to a bench on the left by Chester Creek, where you can sit and rest.

3.1 Pass a small pond and cross a bridge over the creek.

3.2 Pass under the Lake Otis Parkway; Davenport Field is on your right.

3.75 Turn left at the fork and travel past Tikishla Park. Shortly after the park, turn right toward Goose Lake.

3.8 Cross a bridge. Turn right at the trail fork and head uphill and over Northern Lights Boulevard.

4.0 When the trail T's, turn right. (Option: Turn left to go to Russian Jack Park.)

4.1 Arrive at Goose Lake and pavilion.

4.9 Turn left onto UAA Drive.

5.1 Reach the trailhead for Campbell Creek Trail, your turnaround point.

10.2 Arrive back at the trailhead.

18 Campbell Creek Trail

The Campbell Creek Trail stretches from south Anchorage near Minnesota Drive and Dimond Boulevard and heads northeast toward Tudor Road. This popular multipurpose trail follows the scenic Campbell Creek, making it an excellent year-round recreational trail for fishing, picnicking, kids, families, hikers, bicycling, dog walkers, and winter skiers. Numerous access points along the entire trail make it easily accessible from many Anchorage neighborhoods. Campbell Creek is an important watershed and provides excellent salmon viewing, wildlife habitat, and natural flood control.

Distance: 7.4 miles one-way; 14.8 miles out and back

Approximate hiking time: 3 to 4 hours one-way; 7 to 9 hours out and back

Difficulty: Easy

Elevation gain: Negligible

Trail surface: Paved

Best season: Year-round

Other trail users: Walkers, runners, and cyclists; cross-country skiers in winter

Canine compatibility: Leashed dogs permitted

Fees and permits: No fees or permits required

Maps: Anchorage Trail and Parks Map: http://munimaps.muni.org/trails/reference.htm

Trail contacts: Anchorage Park Foundation, 3201 C Street, Suite 111, Anchorage 99503; (907) 274-1003; https://anchorage-parkfoundation.org/; e-mail info@anchorageparkfoundation.org

Special considerations: None

Finding the trailhead: Coming from downtown Anchorage, head south on the Seward Highway. Exit on Dimond Boulevard and head west, traveling approximately 2 miles. Cross over Minnesota Drive and go through the stoplight at the intersection of Dimond Boulevard,

Victor Road, and Northwood Street. The parking lot is immediately on your right; a sign reads Campbell Creek Greenbelt. Walk back across the bridge on Dimond and turn left onto Northwood Street, where the paved trail begins. GPS: N61 08.269 / W149 55.581

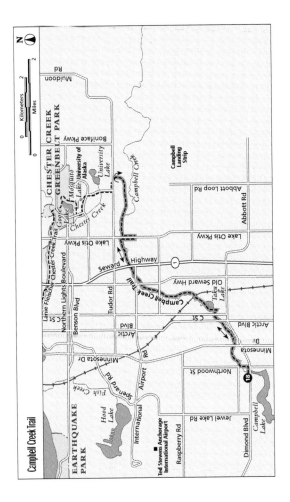

The Hike

The Campbell Creek Trail is easily accessible from numerous points in the many neighborhoods that skirt the trail's 7.4-mile run, making it heavily used and well populated. The multipurpose paved trail stretches from south Anchorage to the northeast side. Start the trail by parking in the main parking lot, located on the north side of Dimond Boulevard just past Minnesota Drive, where there is ample parking. Another parking area, large enough for a couple of cars, is located on Northwood Street, right at the beginning of the paved trail.

The trail heads slightly downhill and quickly comes to one of many bridge crossings that safely take you over the meandering and winding Campbell Creek. After approximately 0.9 mile, cross under Minnesota Drive as you start heading in a northeasterly direction across town. Almost the entire trail follows the creek and runs through beautiful stands of birch-spruce trees. Moose, waterfowl, and other birds are common along the trail. About 0.6 mile after Minnesota Drive, you will cross under Arctic Boulevard, and 0.3 mile beyond here you will come to a bike sign where you need to turn right and cross a bridge. After 2.0 miles of travel, pass Taku Lake on your right. You will cross Campbell Creek a seemingly endless number of times, pass under the major north–south streets of Anchorage, and also cross under the Alaska Railroad.

After about a half-mile, come to a T in the trail with a large signpost in the center. Turn left and continue on the paved path. Cross the creek a couple more times and reach a street crossing. Proceed across with caution. At approximately 4.1 miles, cross under the Old Seward Highway and come to an area with several restaurants and retail businesses you might want to take time to check out. This is a popular stopping area for tour buses.

After approximately 4.4 miles the paved maintained trail ends. Turn left and head across the bridge onto a narrow dirt path. The paved trail begins again on the other side of the Seward Highway. The dirt path follows directly along the shoreline of the creek and under the highway. The path is wet and head clearance is quite low, so be cautious as you work your way to the other side of the highway. Once on the other side, hike out onto Rakof Avenue and travel 2 blocks east. The paved trail begins again on your right at approximately 4.7 miles.

You pass one more lake, Waldron Lake, on your left. This lake provides some good opportunities for viewing different types of waterfowl. The trail follows around and comes out on East 47th Street and heads directly into Lake Otis Boulevard. Follow the crossing signs that take you under Lake Otis Boulevard rather than trying to cross the roadway at this point, where crossing is very dangerous. The Waldron Drive underpass is slightly out of your way, but is a much safer choice.

Once on the other side, the trail goes through a scenic park, crosses a couple more bridges, and passes the Chuck Albrecht Softball Complex. After another half-mile or so, Campbell Creek Trail ends at Tudor Road. Cross Tudor and the trail will join the Lanie Fleischer Chester Creek Trail.

Miles and Directions

0.0 Begin at the trailhead and main parking lot. (Option: Use the small parking area on Northwood Street.)

0.3 Reach one of many bridge crossings over Campbell Creek.

0.9 Cross under Minnesota Drive.

1.5 Cross under Arctic Boulevard.

1.8 Turn right at a bike sign and cross a bridge. Soon, cross under C Street.

2.0 Pass Taku Lake on your right.

2.5 Cross under the Alaska Railroad and over Little Campbell Creek.

3.3 Cross a bridge.

4.1 Cross under Old Seward Highway.

4.25 Cross under International Airport Road.

4.4 The paved trail ends at the Seward Highway. Turn left and cross a bridge onto a dirt path.

4.7 The paved trail begins again.

5.9 Travel past Waldron Lake on your left.

7.4 The trail ends at the Tudor Road trailhead. (Option: Cross Tudor Road to connect with the Lanie Fleischer Chester Creek Trail.)

14.8 Return to the trailhead if hiking out and back.

19 Tony Knowles Coastal Trail

Named for former Alaska governor Tony Knowles, who served from 1981 to 1987, the Tony Knowles Coastal Trail is one of three greenbelt trails located in Anchorage. The multipurpose trail connects the north part of downtown to Kincaid Park in the south and engages various users, including bikers, hikers, dog walkers, runners, and winter skiers. Even though the trail spans 11.0 miles each way, it is easily picked up from several points in the city, so you can enjoy any segment and hike as little or as much of the trail as you desire. The trail provides extraordinary views of downtown Anchorage, the Chugach Mountains, Denali (Mount McKinley), Mount Susitna (Sleeping Lady), and Fire Island. In addition to a lot of other trail users, you are very likely to encounter moose on the trail. The entire trail is paved and mostly easy, except for the last mile, which has a steady hill climb as you approach Kincaid Park.

Distance: 22.0 miles out and back, with multiple access/exit points and options for shortening the hike

Approximate hiking time: 10 to 12 hours out and back for entire trail

Difficulty: Easy to moderate over both flat and hilly terrain

Elevation gain: 117 feet

Trail surface: Pavement

Best season: Year-round

Other trail users: Walkers, runners, cyclists, cross-country skiers

Canine compatibility: Leashed dogs permitted

Fees and permits: No fees or permits required

Maps: USGS Anchorage; Anchorage Trail and Parks Map, http://munimaps.muni.org/trails/reference.htm

Trail contacts: Anchorage Park Foundation, 3201 C Street, Suite 111, Anchorage 99503; (907)

274-1003; https://anchorage-parkfoundation.org/; e-mail info@ anchorageparkfoundation.org.

Special considerations: None

Finding the trailhead: The Tony Knowles Coastal Trail technically begins in downtown Anchorage at the intersection of Second Avenue and H Street. However, more people begin the trail at Elderberry Park at Fifth Avenue and N Street because parking is more readily available at this location. To find Second and H Street, follow Fifth Avenue west through downtown Anchorage. Turn north onto H Street, which becomes Christiansen Drive. Head downhill and turn left at the next intersection, which is Second Avenue; the trailhead is just ahead. GPS: N61 13.234 / W149 53.851

To go to Elderberry Park, continue west on Fifth Avenue toward Cook Inlet. Continue across L Street and head down a steep hill. Parking is on your right.

The Hike

Probably the best-known multipurpose trail in the Anchorage area, the Tony Knowles Coastal Trail is considered a real gem. The trail essentially follows along Cook Inlet in a north–south direction and connects downtown Anchorage and Kincaid Park. Expect to encounter various types of wildlife along the trail. Moose in particular are common and should be taken very seriously when they are on or near the trail. Be sure to slow down, stop, and even wait until the trail is clear. Moose are not tame and can be very dangerous.

The trail is easy to follow, and most people who want to complete the entire trail out and back travel by bike. If you're ambitious, it can be done as a long day hike. However, the trail's many access points within the city make it easy to pick up and walk as much or as little as you desire.

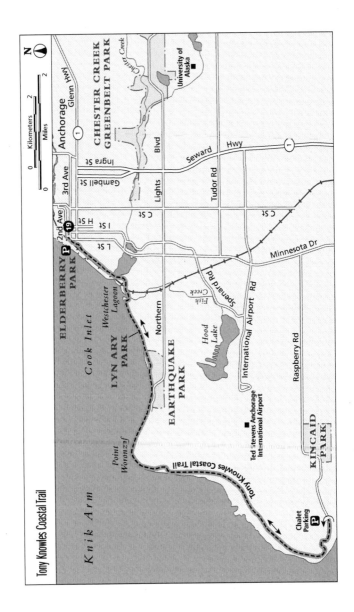

Tony Knowles Coastal Trail

Beginning the trail at Second Avenue and H Street, the Alaska Railroad and the Port of Anchorage are on your right. Cross a wooden bridge and follow the path toward the water. You quickly come to Elderberry Park on your right and the historic Oscar Anderson House. The trail heads slightly downhill and through a tunnel. This is a busy trail, and it is important to stay on your side of the trail and use caution in blind spots.

As you ascend slightly and wind to the left, there are good views of the mudflats and Point MacKenzie across the water. The trail crosses through two tunnels and passes the west side of Westchester Lagoon. It turns and crosses a bridge over a wetland area and Ship Creek and then travels along the water's edge, with some good opportunities to view various species of wading birds and waterfowl.

During the next several miles you will have plenty of opportunities to see some of Anchorage's best parks. Lyn Ary Park is a great little park with picnic facilities, a playground, and tennis courts. Earthquake Park is just before the 4.0-mile point. This area dropped more than 30 feet during the famous 9.2-scale Good Friday earthquake of March 1964. The trail winds through the park, which has several interpretive panels and a monument. Just beyond Earthquake Park is Airport Park, with extraordinary views of the downtown Anchorage skyline and mountain views across Knik Arm.

Point Woronzof is a bit more than a mile up the trail. This popular family stopping place has a beach and bluffs to explore, and offers great views of Sleeping Lady and, on clear days, Mount McKinley.

From this point on, as you approach Kincaid Park, the trail is heavily forested. About 2.6 miles beyond Point Woronzof, you will come to a bridge over a small gorge. All along, you can't help but notice the airline jets and the Ted Stevens Anchorage International Airport. For approximately the last mile, follow a steep, steady incline as you come to the trail's end at the chalet at Kincaid Park.

Miles and Directions

0.0   Start at Second Avenue and H Street in downtown Anchorage.

0.3   Pass Elderberry Park on your right and the historic Oscar Anderson House; go through a tunnel.

1.1   Pass under the Alaska Railroad and cross a bridge; turn right to stay on the trail. (Option: Turn left to pick up the Lanie Fleischer Chester Creek Trail.)

1.5   Cross a bridge over a marshy area, go through a tunnel, and head toward Fish Creek.

2.5   Arrive at Lyn Ary Park.

3.6   Reach a large four-way intersection and archway; Earthquake Park is on your right. (Option: Turn left to reach the Earthquake Park parking lot.)

4.1   Pass Airport Park and a large gravel parking lot with views of the Anchorage skyline.

5.2   Arrive at Point Woronzof.

7.8   Cross a bridge over a small gorge.

11.0   Reach trail's end at Kincaid Park. Unless you have arranged for a shuttle, retrace your steps.

22.0   Arrive back at the Second Avenue and H Street trailhead.

20　Ship Creek Trail

Ship Creek Trail is not one of the most well-known trails in the area, but it's a great trail to check out, and not to be missed. It is an important part of the Anchorage Greenbelt Trails system, and can also be accessed from the popular Tony Knowles Coastal Trail. The easy-to-follow paved path follows Ship Creek for the entire length of the trail. The trail presents views of the Chugach Mountains and downtown Anchorage, white birch, berry picking, birding opportunities, and wildflowers along the trail's edge to the north, and an industrial setting to the south. If you want to see salmon when they are running, this is the trail to do so. From July through September salmon are easily spotted swimming upstream.

Distance: 5.2 miles out and back
Approximate hiking time: 2 to 3 hours
Difficulty: Easy
Elevation gain: Negligible
Trail surface: Paved
Seasons: Year-round
Other trail users: Walkers, runners, and cyclists; cross-country skiers in winter
Canine compatibility: Leashed dogs permitted

Fees and permits: Parking fees in public lots
Maps: Anchorage Trail and Parks Map, http://munimaps.muni.org/trails/reference.htm
Trail contacts: Anchorage Park Foundation, 3201 C Street, Suite 111, Anchorage 99503; (907) 274 1003; https://anchorage-parkfoundation.org/; e-mail info@anchorageparkfoundation.org
Special considerations: None

Finding the trailhead: Coming from downtown Anchorage from Fifth Avenue, head north on E Street, and veer right onto West Second Avenue, which becomes North C Street. This will go past the Alaska

Railroad depot and the Alaska Railroad corporate office building. Turn right onto East Ship Creek Avenue to the parking lot. The trailhead is located at the North C Street bridge, which is behind the Alaska Geographic Association and the Ulu Factory. This trail can also be accessed from the Tony Knowles Coastal Trail. GPS: N61 13.411 / W149 53.269

The Hike

The city of Anchorage has one of the best urban trail systems found anywhere in the entire United States. Ship Creek Trail is one of four trails that are part of this greenbelt system. It is located on the north side of Anchorage and follows directly along Ship Creek and ends at Tyson Elementary School. The illuminated paved trail is also a popular biking trail.

Begin at the trailhead located at the North C Street bridge. As you head eastward on the trail, you will pass by a popular salmon-fishing area. Here you can see the salmon, generally from July through September, swimming upstream to spawn. The banks of the creek will be lined with anglers working the waters. The depth of this stream is directly related to the tide; during low tide you will see shorebirds flitting along the mudflats in the area. Various ducks, geese, godwit, turnstones, and several species of sandpipers are common, particularly during the spring and fall. Another 0.25 mile up the trail you will pass by the Knik Arm Power Plant dam on your left. This is a good stopping point to view upstream and look for salmon and wild birds.

Throughout the trail you will cross several bridges. At approximately Mile 1.5, the trail will loop up and over the Alaska Railroad train trestle and Ship Creek. This is a large bridge with equally big views.

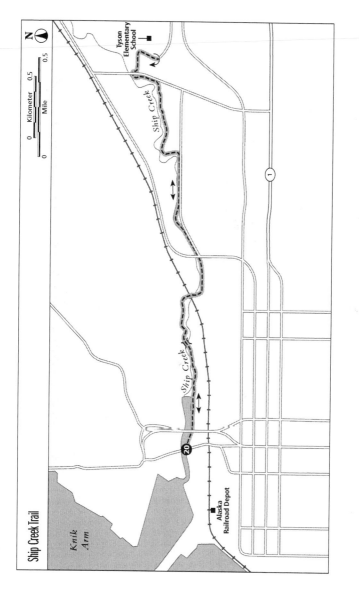

Ship Creek Trail

N

0   Kilometer   0.5
0   Mile   0.5

Knik
Arm

Ship Creek

Ship Creek

Tyson
Elementary
School

Alaska
Railroad Depot

20

1

The trail concludes next to Tyson Elementary School. As with all Anchorage trails, always use caution and be aware of wildlife such as bears and moose which frequently use the same trails that people do. Even in downtown Anchorage, wildlife abounds. From here, head back on the same path to the parking area.

Miles and Directions

0.0 Start at Ship Creek Trailhead.

0.6 Reach the first of several bridge crossings.

0.8 Bridge crossing.

1.5 Bridge crossing.

2.2 Bridge crossing.

2.6 End at Tyson Elementary School. Retrace your steps along same path.

5.2 Arrive back at trailhead.

THE TEN ESSENTIALS OF HIKING

Whether you plan to be gone for a couple of hours or several months, make sure to pack these items. Become familiar with these items and know how to use them.

1. Appropriate Footwear
Happy feet make for pleasant hiking. Think about traction, support, and protection when selecting well-fitting shoes or boots.

2. Navigation
While phones and GPS units are handy, they aren't always reliable in the backcountry; consider carrying a paper map and compass as a backup and know how to use them.

3. Water (and a way to purify it)
As a guideline, plan for half a liter of water per hour in moderate temperatures/terrain. Carry enough water for your trip and know where and how to treat water while you're out on the trail.

4. Food
Pack calorie-dense foods to help fuel your hike, and carry an extra portion in case you are out longer than expected.

5. Rain Gear & Dry-Fast Layers
The weatherman is not always right. Dress in layers to adjust to changing weather and activity levels. Wear moisture-wicking clothes and carry a warm hat.

6. Safety Items (light, fire, and a whistle)
Have means to start an emergency fire, signal for help, and see the trail and your map in the dark.

7. First Aid Kit
Supplies to treat illness or injury are only as helpful as your knowledge of how to use them. Take a class to gain the skills needed to administer first aid and CPR.

8. Knife or Multi-Tool
With countless uses, a multi-tool can help with gear repair and first aid.

9. Sun Protection
Sunscreen, sunglasses, and sun-protective clothing should be used in every season regardless of temperature or cloud cover.

10. Shelter
Protection from the elements in the event you are injured or stranded is necessary. A lightweight, inexpensive space blanket is a great option.

Find other helpful resources at AmericanHiking.org/hiking-resources.